1

Living Waters
Signs of the Times

Anne Marie Mongoven, O.P., Ph.D.
Santa Clara University

Maureen Gallagher, Ph.D.

Liturgical Contributor
Rita Claire Dorner, O.P., Ph.D.
Santa Clara University

Consultants
The Reverend Gerard Sloyan
Jean Marie Hiesberger

General Editor
Eileen Anderson

TABOR PUBLISHING
Allen, Texas

Special Thanks

Tabor Publishing wishes to acknowledge the invaluable contributions of **Greer Gordon, Ph.D.,** Regis College, Weston, Massachusetts. Dr. Gordon's sensitivities to the needs of our multicultural communities assisted greatly in the development of the final manuscript of *Living Waters 1.*

The contributions of **James Bitney, M.A.,** are also gratefully acknowledged. Mr. Bitney shares his training and experience in sacramental theology and family catechesis in the "Family Matters" pages.

NIHIL OBSTAT
Rev. Glenn D. Gardner, J.C.D.
Censor Librorum

IMPRIMATUR
† Most Rev. Charles V. Grahmann
Bishop of Dallas

November 8, 1991

The *Nihil Obstat* and *Imprimatur* are official declarations that the work contains nothing contrary to Faith and Morals. It is not implied thereby that those granting the *Nihil Obstat* and *Imprimatur* agree with the contents, statements, or opinions expressed.

Copyright © 1992 by Tabor Publishing, a division of RCL Enterprises, Inc.

All rights reserved. No part of this book shall be reproduced or transmitted in any form or by any means, electronic or mechanical, including photocopying, recording, or by any information or retrieval system, without written permission from the Publisher.

Send all inquiries to:
Tabor Publishing
200 East Bethany Drive
Allen, Texas 75002-3804

ISBN 0-7829-0010-0

6 7   98

ACKNOWLEDGMENTS
The Scripture on page 130 is taken from *The New American Bible with Revised New Testament* Copyright © 1986 by the Confraternity of Christian Doctrine, Washington, D.C., and is used by permission of copyright owner. All rights reserved.

Excerpts from the English translation of *The Roman Missal* © 1973, International Committee on English in the Liturgy, Inc. All rights reserved.

BOOK DESIGN
Tabor Publishing

PHOTOGRAPHY
Full Photographics   All photography except:
Scala/Art Resource, New York   Inside front and back covers
The Stock Market/Pedro Coll   73 (top)
The Stock Market/Gabe Palmer, 1986   73 (bottom)

ILLUSTRATIONS
Christy J. Hellman   5, 12, 165
Paula Lawson   6-11, 13, 16-17, 19-24, 28-29, 35-40, 64-65, 94-95, 97, 102, 120-33, 136, 141
Tricia Legault   91-93, 96, 150-51
Karen McDonald   66-67, 75, 76-79 (border), 153, 158, 168-69
Darren McKee   14-15, 18, 42-46, 48-49, 58, 70-72, 74, 76-80, 98-101, 104-8, 160-61, 163
Nancy Munger   50-57, 68, 109-14, 148-49, 152, 156-57, 170
Jennifer Andrew Pickett   41, 63, 164
John Stevens   30

Contents

Chapter 1:	**NAMING**	5
	Family Matters	4
Our Lives:	What Is Your Name?	7
God's Word:	The Name of Jesus	13
The Church:	My Name Is "Catholic"	19
We Pray:	The Day I Was Named (Baptism)	25
	Remembering	31
Chapter 2:	**BEING SPECIAL**	33
	Family Matters	34
Our Lives:	Special People, Special Times	35
God's Word:	Jesus Is Special (Jesus and the Children)	41
The Church:	The Father and the Holy Spirit Are Special (The Lord's Prayer)	47
We Pray:	Sunday Is Our Special Day (Mass, "Alleluia!")	53
	Remembering	59
Chapter 3:	**HANDS ARE FOR HELPING**	61
	Family Matters	62
Our Lives:	Using Our Hands	63
God's Word:	Jesus' Helping Hands (The Good Samaritan)	69
The Church:	Hands That Help Others (Francis of Assisi, Louise de Marillac)	75
We Pray:	We Pray with Our Hands	81
	Remembering	87

Chapter 4:	**EARS ARE FOR HEARING**	89
	Family Matters	90
Our Lives:	Listening	91
God's Word:	We Listen to Stories about Jesus	97
The Church:	We Listen to Jesus' Teachings (The Great Commandment)	103
We Pray:	We Listen at Mass	109
	Remembering	115
Chapter 5:	**EYES ARE FOR SEEING**	117
	Family Matters	118
Our Lives:	What Can We See?	119
God's Word:	We Can See What God Has Made (Creation)	125
The Church:	We Can See the Church (The people in the Church help others)	131
We Pray:	We See Our Parish at Mass	137
	Remembering	143
Chapter 6:	**LIFE IS GOOD**	145
	Family Matters	146
Our Lives:	We Are Alive	147
God's Word:	God Gives Us Life	153
The Church:	Jesus Loved Life	159
We Pray:	Praise God for Life (Morning and night prayers)	165
	Remembering	171
The Liturgical Year		
	Advent/Christmas	172
	Easter	174
Prayers		176

Our Lives

God's Word

The Church

We Pray

These symbols represent the four signs of catechesis as found in *The General Catechetical Directory* and *The National Catechetical Directory*.

Family Matters

Spreading Our Story

What's in a name? Plenty. Children know this—almost instinctively. Probably the first word your child uttered was a name: "Mama" or "Papa." Then, as your child grew, he or she discovered—even *gave*— names to the world and its objects. Naming helped your child understand and appreciate the wonderful world around him or her.

What's in a name? Plenty. Parents know this. Think of the hours you spent contemplating what name to give your child. You recognized that a name would both establish your child in a family and shape your child's identity as he or she grew. Think, too, about the way a name evokes faith. For instance, you wouldn't trust your savings to an institution named "Fast Freddie's Mobile Bank," would you? Not likely.

What's in a name? Plenty. The faith community knows this. That's why the first thing we, as "Church," ask parents of a newborn is "What name do you give your child?" That's why we baptize our children in the *name* of the triune God. That's why we begin all our prayers in God's *name,* and end them by wrapping them in the *name* of Christ Jesus, "the God-sent One who loves and saves us." And that's why we *name* ourselves Catholic Christians, "followers of Christ who are open to all."

The name of God is Love.

What's in a name? Children, parents, and the faith community all know that naming leads to identity, identity to understanding, understanding to appreciation, appreciation to faith, and faith to love. And the name of God is *Love.* And the story of our relationship to God is a love story— the greatest ever told.

Celebrating Our Story

Set aside a time to share the story of how and why you gave your child his or her name. Make it a real story time. If you wish, begin with those almost magic words: "Once upon a time . . ." Afterward, cut the letters of your child's first name out of construction paper, mix them up, and have— or help—your child put them together.

Take time to explain to your child what his or her name means. (You can find the meaning of most names in the library. But remember to share the special or unique meaning your child's name may have for you and your family.) Likewise, tell what your first name means. Finally, if possible, explain what your family name means.

Post the letters of your child's name on the door to his or her room or at another place in your home where everyone can view them. Over the next few weeks, have your child draw portraits of people near and dear. Help your child print the names of these people on their portraits. Let your child post these pictures under his or her name to make a "portrait gallery of names."

You might also share a book about names with your child, for example, *I Have Four Names for My Grandfather* by Kathryn Lasky.

Conclude your celebration by blessing your child. Place your hand on your child's head or shoulders—or, better, cradle your child's face in your hands—and bless him or her by name:

_____*(Name)*_____, God bless you, keep you, and help you live up to your name.

Let this blessing become a regular part of your prayer with your child. Have your child bless you as well.

© 1992 Tabor Publishing
Permission to duplicate is granted.

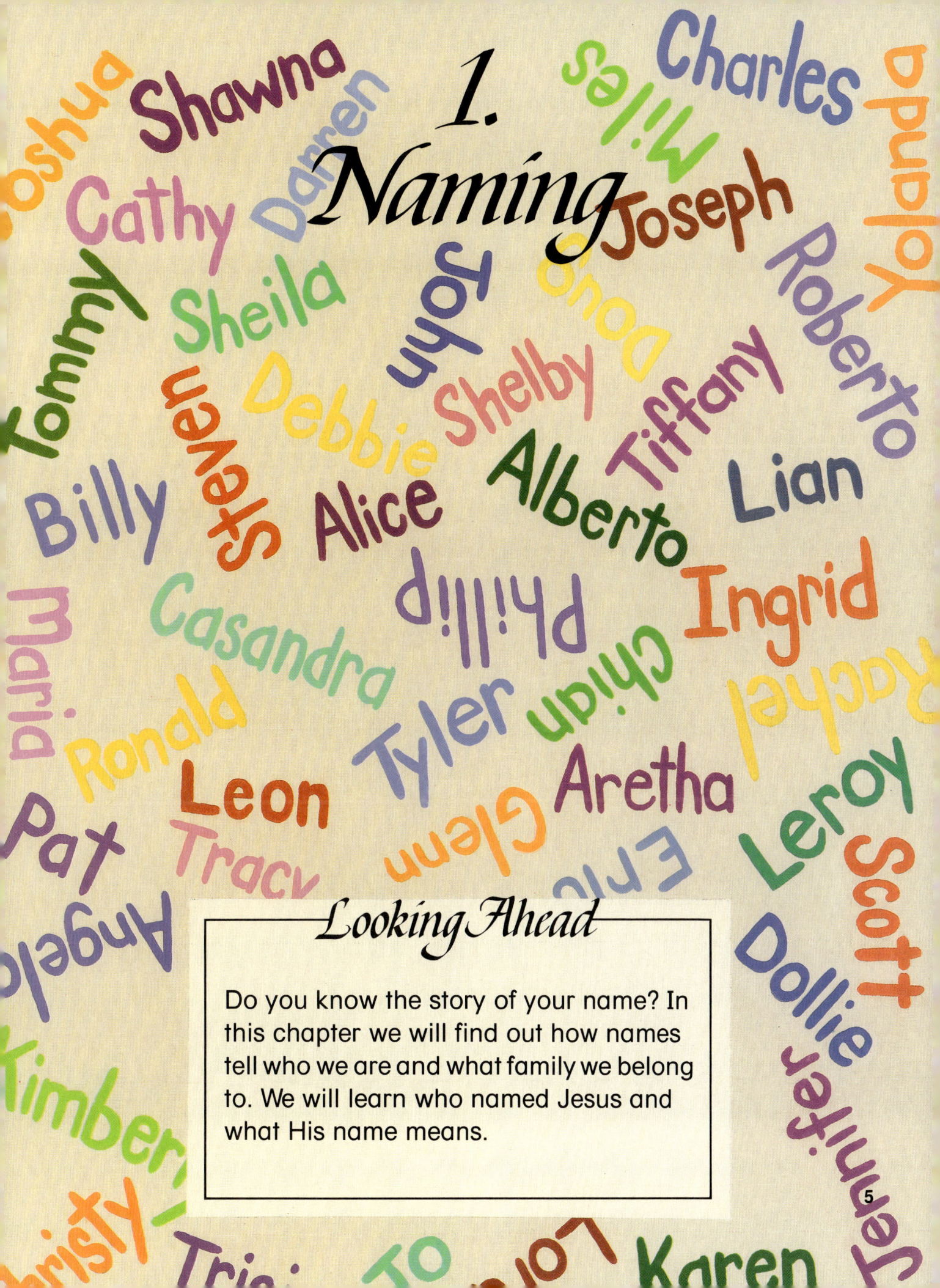

PART ONE
What Is Your Name?

Read with Me

What is your name?
Print your first name and draw yourself in this space.

The Two Emilys

The school bus arrived with all the excited first graders. The children in Ms. Arnold's group found their teacher waiting in front of her room with a big smile for each of them. The first day was so exciting!

Ms. Arnold greeted each of the children by name. "Good morning, Emily. My name is Ms. Arnold," she said.

"Good morning, Ms. Arnold," said Emily.

"Good morning, Ms. Arnold," said another little girl named Emily.

Ms. Arnold laughed and said, "I can see we have two Emilys in our group. How will we know who is who?"

How would you solve the problem of the two Emilys?

Do you know anyone
with the same name as yours?
If so, how does that make you feel?
If not, how does that make you feel?

"Oh, Ms. Arnold, I know how you can tell who we are," laughed the first Emily. "My last name is Wilson. I'm Emily Wilson."

"And my family name is Conti. I'm Emily Conti," laughed the other Emily.

"Well now!" smiled Ms. Arnold. "What wonderful family names you both have. Now we know the two Emilys!"

You have a first name and
a family name.
Your first name tells who you are.
Your family name tells what family you belong to.
Ask someone to help you print your family name here.

_____

Tell who belongs to your family.

Nicknames are special names, too.
Sometimes, they are short names,
like Bill
or Kate.

Sometimes, nicknames are names
that tell about a person,
like Curly
or Speedy.

Do you have a nickname?
Tell us about it.

Roberto had a special nickname, "Flaco."
<u>Flaco</u> means "Slim" in Spanish.
Roberto was tall and thin for his age.
Roberto did not like his nickname—
until the day his dog, Dusty, got lost.

Roberto's dog, Dusty, had run away down the street. Everyone joined in looking for Dusty. Suddenly Rosa spotted Dusty under Mr. Arimoto's front porch.

Dusty was so scared that he would not come out from under the porch by himself. He would not move!

Roberto was thin enough to crawl under the porch. He rescued Dusty!

"Wow!" shouted Rosa. "Flaco the Fantastic!"

Roberto likes his nickname, now.

All our names are special!

Sometimes we give names
to our toys or pets.
The names show that they belong to us.

Name these pets and toys.
Tell why you chose the names.

Let Us Pray

Catechist: Let us begin our prayer.
God knows each of us by name.
Let us celebrate
by praying for each other by name.
As we pray for you, put your name sign
on the naming tree.
Let us pray for _____(name)_____.

All: God bless _____(name)_____.

Catechist: Let us pray for our friends.

Children: God bless _____(name)_____.

Catechist: Let us bow our heads
and pray for God's blessing.
God bless us
and all the people in the world.

Children: Amen.

PART TWO
The Name of Jesus

Read with Me

Families choose special names
for their children.
Sometimes we are named after our
grandparents or aunts or uncles.
Sometimes families choose names
with special meanings.

> Matthew means "gift from God."
> Sarah means "princess."
> Kiala means "one who cares."

Tell us the story
of why you were given your name.
Do you know what your name means?

Listen to find out how a baby was named in the Bible. The Bible is God's storybook.

Mary and Elizabeth were cousins. They were good friends, too. Mary and Elizabeth both were going to have babies. Mary went to visit Elizabeth to help with the new baby.
(From Luke 1:39-40)

Elizabeth had a son. She named him "John." <u>John</u> means "God is good."
(From Luke 1:57-60)

Can you guess why Elizabeth named her baby "John"?

Can you imagine what Mary and Elizabeth are saying? Act out Mary's visit with Elizabeth.

When John grew up, he became a preacher. He told the people that they should love God and one another. When they promised they would try, he baptized them. The people began to call him "John the Baptist." (From Luke 3:3–4)

Can you guess why the people gave John this name?

Use this drawing to tell about John the Baptist.

Soon Mary had her baby, too.
Mary named her Son "Jesus."
The name <u>Jesus</u> means "God saves."
Jesus saves us from being alone.
That is why one of Jesus' names
is "Savior."
Jesus tells us
that God is always with us.
(From Luke 2:21)

When Jesus grew up, He traveled about, telling the people how much God loved them. Jesus showed the people how to love God and one another. So some people called Jesus by another name. They named Him "the Christ." (From Luke 9:20)

Christ means "the One sent from God." Jesus Christ was sent by God. Jesus Christ is God's own Son.

Find and color the name of God's Son, Jesus Christ.

Let Us Pray

Catechist: Let us begin our prayer.
Let us open our hearts to God
as Elizabeth, John the Baptist,
and Mary did.
Let us sing our prayer to Jesus.

Children: Jesus, You are our Savior.
You are the One sent by God.

Catechist: We believe that Mary is the Mother
of God's Son, Jesus.

Children: Jesus, You are our Savior.
You are the One sent by God.

Catechist: We believe that Jesus Christ saves us
from being alone.

Children: Jesus, You are our Savior.
You are the One sent by God.

Catechist: We believe that Jesus is always
with us.

Children: Jesus, You are our Savior.
You are the One sent by God.

Catechist: In the name of Jesus, I bless you.
Children: Amen.

PART THREE
My Name Is "Catholic"

Read with Me

Finish these faces.
Make them look like children you know.

Tell us the names of the children in your picture.

All these children belong
to one large family.
We are all God's children.
God made us all.
We are called "children of God."
All of us are sisters and brothers
in God's family.

Many of us have another name.
We are called "Christian."
We are named after Jesus Christ.

Color this "I am a Christian" name sign.

Some of us in the Christian family have another name.
We belong to the Catholic Church.
We call ourselves "Catholic."

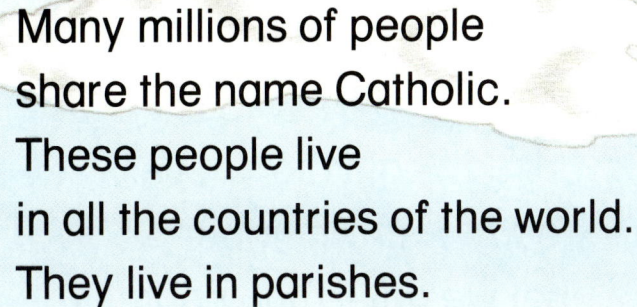

Many millions of people
share the name Catholic.
These people live
in all the countries of the world.
They live in parishes.

Each parish has a name.
Put the name of our parish here.

_____

- -

_____

Tell us the names
of some families you know
who belong to our parish.

Let Us Pray

Catechist: Let us begin our prayer.
Today we remember
that we have many names.
Let us pray for all who are named
"children of God."

Children: God bless us.

Catechist: Let us pray for all who are named Christian.

Children: God bless us.

Catechist: Let us pray for all who are named Catholic.

Children: God bless us.

Catechist: Let us pray for all who belong to _____(name)_____ parish.

Children: God bless us.

Catechist: In the name of Jesus, I bless you.

Children: Amen.

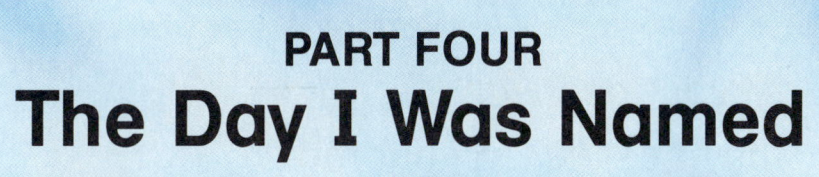

PART FOUR
The Day I Was Named

Read with Me

Can you guess
why this family is so happy?
Their new baby is going to be baptized.
The baby will become a Christian.

At your baptism,
the priest asked your family,
"What name do you give your child?"
Your family told the priest your name.
They said, "Our child is named
_____(name)_____."
The priest baptized you.
You were welcomed
into the Christian family.
You became a Catholic Christian.

At your baptism,
the priest put you in the water
or poured water over your head
and prayed,
  "_____(name)_____, I baptize you
  in the name of the Father,
  and of the Son,
  and of the Holy Spirit."

We are all baptized in the name of God.

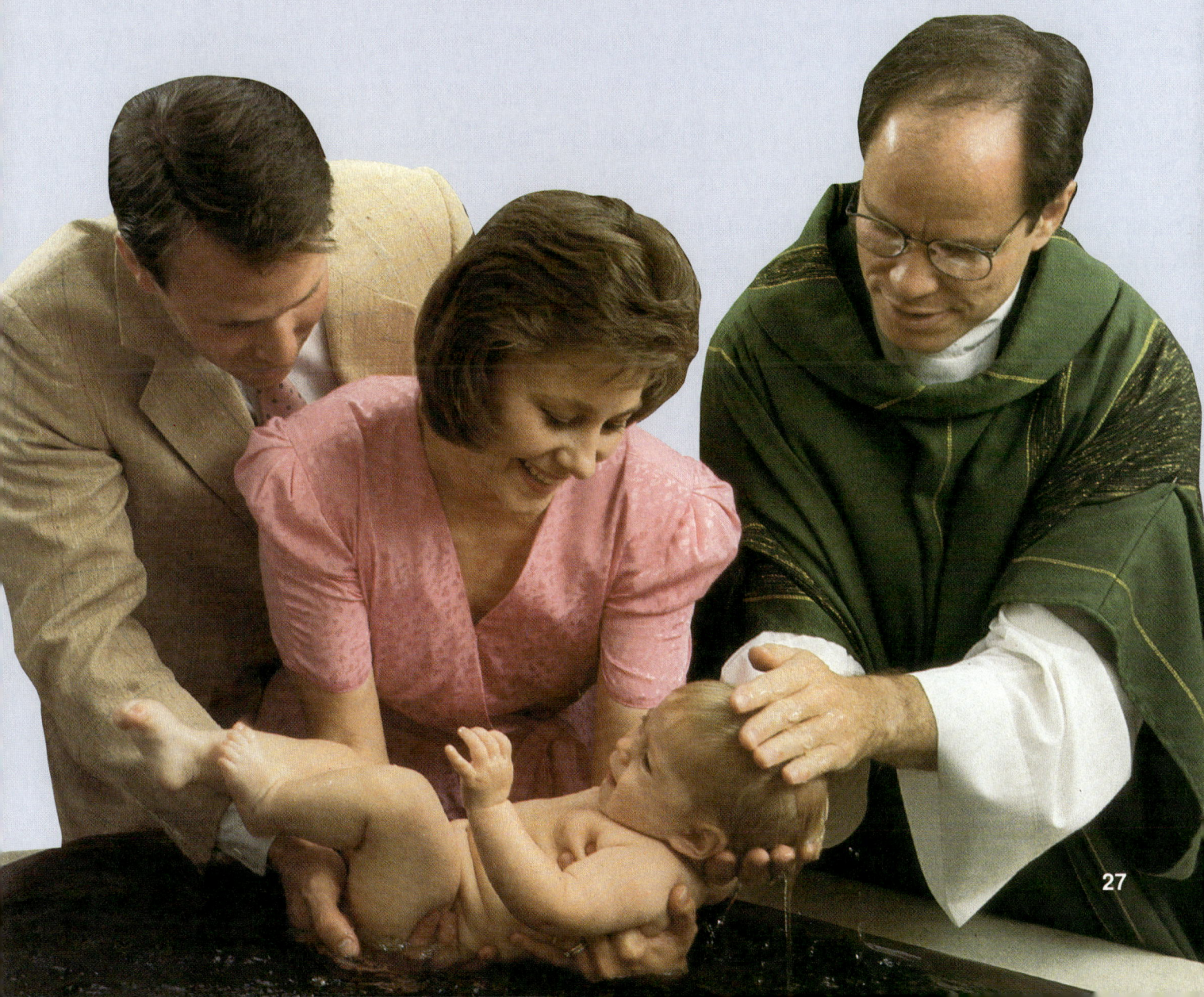

The prayer from your baptism
is a prayer for you to learn.
It is our prayer for naming God.
We begin and end our prayers
with this prayer.
It is called the **Sign of the Cross.**

Can you learn to pray
the **Sign of the Cross?**
When will you pray this prayer?

The Sign of the Cross

We pray,

1   "In the name of the Father,

2   and of the Son,

3 **4**   and of the Holy Spirit.

5   Amen."

Let Us Pray

Catechist: Let us begin with our naming prayer.
All: In the name of the Father,
and of the Son,
and of the Holy Spirit. Amen.
Catechist: Water reminds us of our baptism.
It reminds us of the day we were named.
Sometimes grown-ups are baptized, too.
They have a name already, but they are
baptized in God's name, just as we are.
I am going to bless each of you
with this water.
After I bless you, say, "Amen."
_____(name)_____, I bless you
in the name of the Father,
and of the Son,
and of the Holy Spirit.
Let us close our prayer
with our naming prayer.
All: In the name of the Father,
and of the Son,
and of the Holy Spirit.
Amen.

Remembering

Read with Me

Color the happy face to answer **YES**.
Color the sad face to answer **NO**.

1. Everybody has a name.

2. My name tells what family I belong to.

3. My family gave me my name when I was born.

4. God knows each of us by name.

5. Mary is the mother of God's Son, Jesus.

6. Jesus means "God saves."

7. Jesus Christ was sent by God.

8. Elizabeth named her Son "Jesus."

9. The name <u>John</u> means "God is good."

10. Jesus tells us that God is always with us.

Color the happy face to answer **YES**.
Color the sad face to answer **NO**.

1. All people are children of God.

2. I am glad I am God's child.

3. I am a Christian.

4. Christians are named after Jesus Christ.

5. Jesus Christ is God's own Son.

6. I know the name of the parish I belong to.

7. My family brought me to be baptized.

8. I was baptized in the name of the Father, and of the Son, and of the Holy Spirit.

9. I know how to pray the Sign of the Cross.

10. I believe God loves me.

2. Being Special

Looking Ahead

We are special! In this chapter we will find out why each one of us is special and why some days are special. We will discover why Jesus and the Father and the Holy Spirit are special.

Family Matters

Being Special

Like any good parent, you believe that *your* child truly *is* special. You want your child to realize this, recognize his or her worth, and grow in self-esteem. But what does being special mean?

Being special means being an original.

The whole notion of "specialness" seems to be rooted in the very beginning of things. If you recall the biblical account of the beginning of things, you will remember that God rated all created things "good," with no strings attached. In other words, God favored each and every created thing not because it was different or separate from all others, but because all created things came from the hand of God—all were *originals*. Surely, that's what being special means—*being an original*.

Your duty and delight is to help your child develop and sustain his or her originality (specialness). This is no easy task, for your child will be under great pressure to conform, accommodate, blend in. Unless children very quickly discover a sense of self-worth, they very quickly lose confidence in their originality and abandon it in favor of conventionality.

It is sad to see this happen, especially when you recall that Christians are summoned to live up to their namesake, who was the *absolute* original. Jesus clearly recognized the specialness of children. He saw them not as miniature facsimiles of adults, to be esteemed according to their ability to conform, but as substantial originals of God, to be esteemed "good" with no strings attached.

Your efforts will help your child to treasure his or her own specialness and to become aware of the specialness of all others. Being so aware enables your child not only to be special but to become holy.

Celebrating Specialness

Recognize that your child's specialness is not reserved only for special times. Your child is special *every day*. So here are some do's and don'ts to help you treat your child as someone who is very special.

- Do be free with affirmation.
- Do acknowledge successes as they occur.
- Do encourage your child to respond to approval with simple acknowledgments.
- Don't let your child minimize his or her accomplishments.
- Don't use money or material gifts as rewards for positive behavior.
- Don't give others credit for what your child does.

Draw attention to your child's specialness—to all the new things he or she is learning, to the way he or she treats others, to his or her developing skills. Share these with your child and with God in prayer. Use a prayer like the following to celebrate specialness.

PARENT: Precious God, help us to love all life as You do. Teach us to see that all life is special and good.

ALL: We bless the Lord with shouts of joy. We offer God our praise. We thank the Lord with lives well lived today and all our days.

(Cup your child's face in your hands and say:)

PARENT: _(Child's name)_ , God made you *you*—a special gift of God's precious love. Let's say "Thank You, God."

ALL: Thank You, God.

Conclude by sharing a special food your child enjoys or by sharing a story about specialness, such as *The Mixed-Up Chameleon* by Eric Carle.

© 1992 Tabor Publishing
Permission to duplicate is granted.

PART ONE
Special People, Special Times

Read with Me

Who are these special people?
How do they help us?

Our special people help us to grow.
They teach us new things.
We try to do what they do.
We want to be like them.

Where Is Lian?

"Lian! Chen! Let's go now. I want to get to the market before it closes!"

"I'm ready, Mom," Chen answered, "but I don't know where Lian is. I think she's next door with her friend, Heidi."

"Oh, my," Mom answered, "Heidi and her family left in their car just a few minutes ago. Come, Chen, help me find your sister."

Mom asked Mr. Jackson, who was walking his dog, if he had seen Lian. Chen asked some children who were playing in the park. No one had seen Lian. Mom and Chen even asked Mrs. Davis, who was delivering mail. "I haven't seen Lian around, Mrs. Kwan," she said. "But I'll keep an eye out for her."

Finally, Mom and Chen went home. They had searched the whole neighborhood. They had talked to everyone they could. Still, they had not found Lian.

"We'll have to call the police," Mrs. Kwan said. "I know they will help us."

Soon, Officers Malcolm and Judith arrived at Lian's home. They began to ask a lot of questions about Lian.

Just then the phone rang. It was Mr. MacGregor, the school principal. "I just heard you're looking for Lian. I saw her running toward the bridge over the creek a little while ago," he said.

"The Bridge House!" shouted Chen. "That's our favorite place to play. I bet that's where she is!"

Everyone ran to the little house beside the bridge. There was Lian, surrounded by five little kittens! "Shhh!" whispered Lian. "Heidi's cat just had kittens. And I helped her."

Everyone smiled at Lian. They were so glad she had been found.

What special people helped to find Lian?

What special person do you want to be like when you grow up?
Act out how you can be like that person.

Some days are special, too.
We call some of our special days holidays.
What is your favorite holiday?

Look at the pictures here.
Which holidays do they remind you of?
Tell what you know about each one.

Your birthday is a very special day, too.
What things do you like to do
on your birthday?
Why is it such a special day?
Draw candles on your cake
to show how old you are.

Let Us Pray

Catechist: Let us begin with our naming prayer.
All: In the name of the Father,
and of the Son,
and of the Holy Spirit. Amen.
Catechist: Let us take turns thanking God
for our special people.
Child: This is _____(name)_____.
She/He is special because
_____.
All: Thank You, God, for _____(name)_____.
She/He is a special person.
Catechist: Thank You, God, for _____.
You are all very special people, too.
All: Amen.

PART TWO
Jesus Is Special

Read with Me

Tell a story about someone
who is special to you.
Why is that person so special?
Do you want to be like
your special person? Why?

The Bible tells us about someone
who is very special to us.
Jesus is our very special person.
Jesus loves us all and shows us
how to love one another.

We learn about Jesus from the Bible. Listen to find out what happened when Jesus met a man named Zaccheus.

Zaccheus was cheating the people in his town. So the people would have nothing to do with him.

One day Zaccheus heard Jesus teaching. He knew that Jesus was special. He wanted to know Jesus better.

Jesus loved Zaccheus and wanted to help him change. He told Zaccheus He would have supper at Zaccheus' house. After talking to Jesus, Zaccheus decided to become an honest man. Jesus helped Zaccheus to be honest and to do what was right. (From Luke 19:1–10)

Jesus will help us to be honest, too. Jesus is our very special person.

The Bible tells us about another time when Jesus made friends with someone. Listen to find out what Jesus did.

One day a woman came to the well for water. She was lonely and needed a friend. No one in her town would speak to her.

Jesus asked the woman for a drink of water. He helped the woman to know how much God loved her. The woman listened to Jesus. She learned about God's love for her. She told all the people in the town about how special Jesus is. (From John 4:5–30)

Jesus is our special friend, too. He shows us how much God loves us.

The Bible also tells us how much Jesus loves all children.

One day some parents brought their children to Jesus. They knew that Jesus was special. Jesus' friends tried to send the children away. They thought Jesus was too busy to see the children.

But Jesus didn't think so. He said, "Let the little children come to Me!" Jesus laid His hands on the children and blessed each and every one of them.
(From Luke 18:15–16)

Jesus loves all children everywhere. He helps us to love others, too.

Jesus is our very special person.
He shows us how much God loves us.
He shows us how to be kind
to all people,
even people no one else likes.

Pretend there is a new boy or girl
in our group.
Tell how you will be kind to that child.

Let Us Pray

Catechist: Let us begin with our naming prayer.
All: In the name of the Father,
and of the Son,
and of the Holy Spirit. Amen.
Catechist: Let us stand and listen
to a special story about Jesus (page 44).
"Jesus and the Children"
All sing: "Jesus, You Are Our Savior."
Catechist: _____(Name)_____, Jesus loves you.
You are special.
All: Amen.

PART THREE
The Father and the Holy Spirit Are Special

Read with Me

Each of us has special people
who love us.
Our special people help us to grow.
How do special people help you to grow?
Who would you wish to be like?

Tell how you want to be
like your special person.

God the Father is special to Jesus.
Jesus loves the Father.
Jesus called the Father "Abba."
(From Mark 14:36)

<u>Abba</u> means "Father" in English.
Jesus said, "The Father loves you."

God the Father is very special to us.
Jesus shows us how special
the Father is.

Jesus' friends asked Him how to pray.
Jesus told them to say,

"Our Father, who art in heaven,
hallowed be thy name.
Thy Kingdom come.
Thy will be done on earth
as it is in heaven.
Give us this day our daily bread,
and forgive us our trespasses
as we forgive those who trespass
against us.
And lead us not into temptation,
but deliver us from evil. Amen."
(From Matthew 6:9–13)

We call the prayer Jesus taught us
the **Our Father,**
or the **Lord's Prayer.**
Can you learn this prayer?

God the Holy Spirit is also special
to Jesus.
Before Jesus died,
He said to His friends,
   "I will not leave you alone.
   I will send the Spirit to you."
   (From John 14:16)

The Holy Spirit will be with us always.
The Holy Spirit loves and cares for us.
The Holy Spirit helps us to be happy.
The Holy Spirit is very special to us.

The Holy Spirit is always with us.
The Holy Spirit helps us to love one another.

God the Father, God the Son,
and God the Holy Spirit
are called the Holy Trinity.

Mark the pictures that show
the children being kind and loving.
Tell a story about each of the pictures.

Let Us Pray

Catechist: Let us begin with our naming prayer.
All: In the name of the Father,
and of the Son,
and of the Holy Spirit. Amen.
Catechist: The Father is special.
Jesus, the Son, is special.
Let us join hands and pray together
the prayer to the Father
that Jesus gave us.
All pray: Our Father, who art in heaven . . .
Catechist: Let us pray.
The Holy Spirit is special.
Let us join hands
and pray to the Holy Spirit.
Come, Holy Spirit.
Give us Your gift of kindness.
All: Come, Holy Spirit.
Give us Your gift of kindness.
Catechist: May the Father, the Son,
and the Holy Spirit be with us all.
All: Amen.

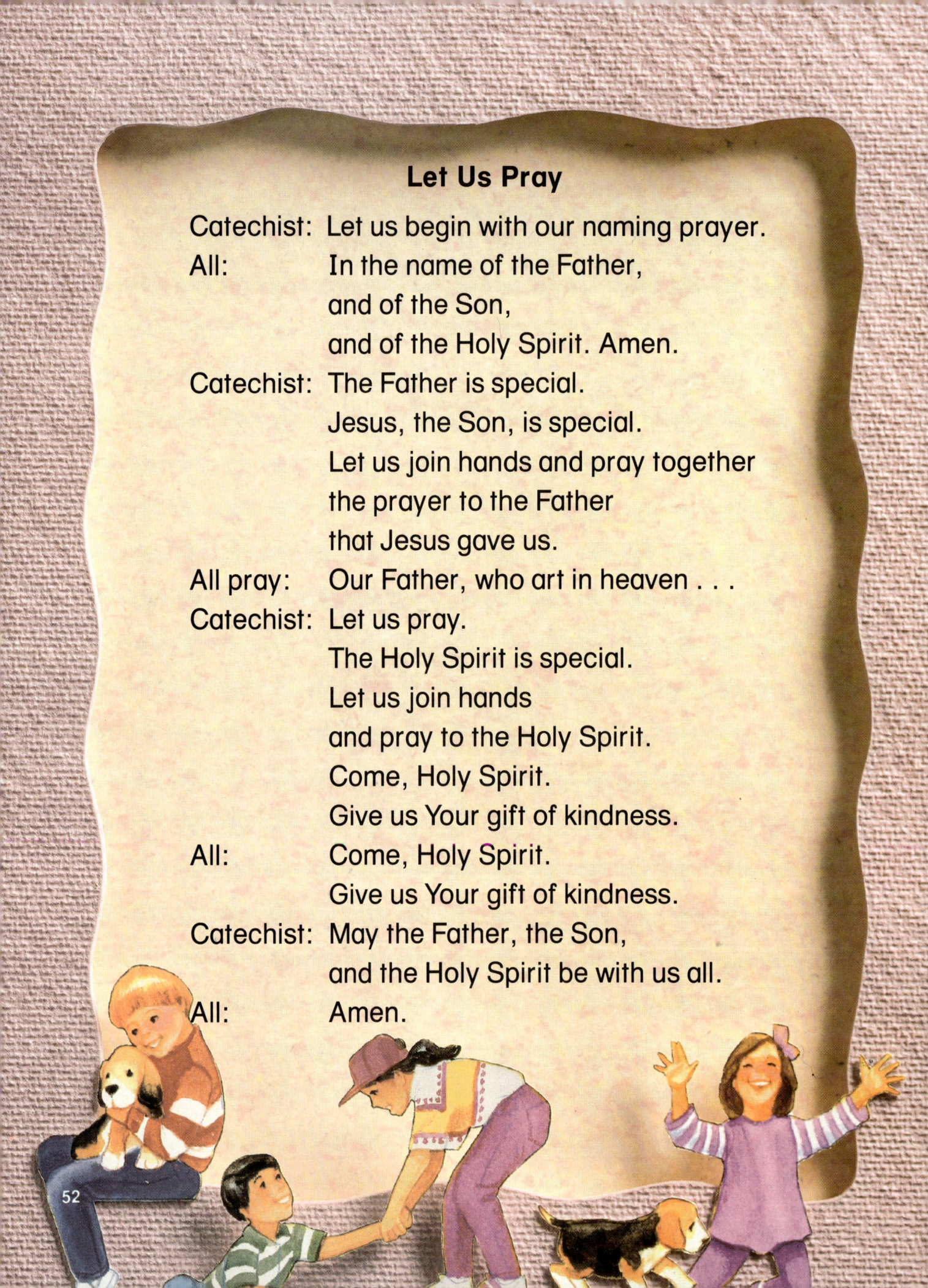

PART FOUR
Sunday Is Our Special Day

Read with Me

Sunday is our special day.
What things do you like to do on Sunday?
Tell what these people are doing together.

For Christians, Sunday is a special day.
It is the Lord's Day.
On Sunday, we celebrate
that Jesus is with us always.
Our parish gathers to give thanks to God.
We call our thanksgiving celebration
the Mass.
The Mass is sometimes called
the Eucharist.
Eucharist means "thanksgiving."

Draw your family
coming to church for Mass.

At Sunday Mass we pray or sing,
"Alleluia! Alleluia!"
Alleluia means "We praise God!"
We praise God at Mass
for giving us Jesus.
Sunday is a very special day.

Color the word Alleluia.
It will remind you to celebrate
our special day.

During the Eucharist,
we listen to Jesus' words.
Someone reads them to us from the gospel.
Gospel means "Good News."
Jesus' words are good news for everyone.

After we listen to the gospel, we say,
"Praise to you, Lord Jesus Christ."

Sunday is a very special day.
Sunday is the day we listen
to the gospel.

Who reads the gospel at Mass
in our parish?

At the end of the Eucharist we hear, "Go in peace to love and serve the Lord." We answer, "Thanks be to God."

Sunday is a very special day. After Mass we go to love and serve others as Jesus did.

Share with your group how you will love and serve others this week.

Let Us Pray

Catechist: Let us begin with our naming prayer.
All: In the name of the Father,
and of the Son,
and of the Holy Spirit. Amen.
All sing: Alleluia! Alleluia!
Catechist: A reading from the gospel:
One day Jesus was walking along the
shore of a lake. He saw two fishermen,
Peter and his brother, Andrew.
They were catching fish with a net.
"Come follow Me," Jesus said.
Peter knew that Jesus was special.
He left his fishing nets
and went with Jesus. (From Mark 1:16–18)
The gospel of the Lord.
All: Praise to you, Lord Jesus Christ.
Catechist: Let us join hands and pray together
the prayer that Jesus gave us,
the **Lord's Prayer.**
All pray: Our Father, who art in heaven . . .
Catechist: May the Father, the Son,
and the Holy Spirit bless us all.
All: Thanks be to God. Amen.

Remembering

Read with Me

Circle the best answer.

1. Special people help me to grow. — **YES** / NO
2. Jesus helped Zaccheus to grow. — **YES** / NO
3. The woman at the well told people how special Jesus is. — **YES** / NO
4. Jesus said He was too busy to see the children. — YES / **NO**
5. <u>Abba</u> means "Holy Spirit." — **YES** / **NO**
6. The prayer that Jesus taught us is called the Lord's Prayer. — **YES** / NO
7. Jesus sent us the Holy Spirit. — **YES** / NO
8. The Holy Spirit helps us to love others. — **YES** / NO
9. Sunday is special because we give thanks to God at Mass. — **YES** / NO
10. <u>Alleluia</u> means "thanksgiving." — YES / **NO**

Circle the best answer.

1. I am a special person. **YES** NO
2. I feel happy when I know Jesus loves me. **YES** NO
3. Jesus said, "Let the children come to Me." **YES** NO
4. We learn about Jesus from newspapers. YES **NO**
5. Jesus shows us how to be kind to all people. **YES** NO
6. I like to share with others. **YES** NO
7. I want to say "thank You" to Jesus for telling us about the Father. **YES** NO
8. The Mass is sometimes called the Eucharist. **YES** NO
9. On Sunday we sing "Alleluia!" because Jesus is with us. **YES** NO
10. The word <u>gospel</u> means "Good News." **YES** NO

3. Hands Are for Helping

Looking Ahead

Little hands! Big hands! Helping hands! In this chapter we will find out how people use their hands to help others. We will learn what Jesus did to show us how to help people with our hands.

Family Matters

Handing On the Faith

What have hands to do with faith and passing on the faith? Much. Jesus made it clear that our faith must be a hands-on faith. Ah! But if there's one thing that sets us to wringing our hands, it's trying to find ways to hand on our faith—to show our children what it means to be "Church." An old rhyme and its accompanying hand gestures can help us do just that.

> Here is the Church.
> Here is the steeple.
> Open the door.
> See all the people.

Our faith must be a hands-on faith.

Here is the steeple. Like a steeple, the Church *points,* but it must never point to *itself* as the event, the person, the revelation, the kingdom. Rather, it must point beyond itself and see itself as a sign of something—of Someone—beyond itself.

Open the door. The Church is *open*—"catholic"—welcoming to all, so that it can recognize, draw out, and utilize what is noble, truthful, and beautiful in every single person. We share in the Church's openness when we engage in hospitable liturgy, concerned catechesis, and encompassing pastoral ministry. We prove our openness by siding with the poor and outcast. We owe our openness to Jesus, who points out that the doors of the Church's openness are hinged with justice and that we must work hard to keep them well oiled.

See all the people. More than anything else, the Church is *people.* As Church, we are more than a group gathered to do good. We are a priestly people, called to set our hands to transforming the world into a place graced. As Church, we can't claim to be the only place where God is, but we can claim—and rightly so—that we are the place where God has promised to *always* be.

Celebrating Hands

> Here is the Church.
> Here is the steeple.
> Open the door.
> See all the people.

That's the Church. That's us. That's our faith, hands down. Teach your child this rhyme. Hand on the faith.

Besides sharing the hand gestures and the rhyme about the Church with your child, there are many ways to celebrate God's gift of hands and all they can do.

- Have a taffy pull.
- Bob for apples—no hands!
- Have a family tug-of-war.
- Mix, knead, bake, and break bread.
- Make a family portrait. Have family members use an ink pad to make thumbprints on a sheet of drawing paper. With pens or pencils, have everyone add features (mouth, eyes, and so on) to complete the portrait.
- Clap hands, snap fingers, make finger puppets.
- Share a story about hands, such as *Here Are My Hands* by Bill Martin Jr. and John Archambault.
- Do a handstand.
- Do a family project. Clean out closets, cupboards, toy chests. Donate unused items to a local charity. Afterward, give everyone a hand (a round of applause).

No matter how you celebrate hands, wrap your family festivity in prayer:

> With joyful hands, now praise the Lord!
> *(Clap hands.)*
>
> With hands, share God's peace, too.
> *(Shake hands with one another.)*
>
> With joyful hands, now praise the Lord!
> *(Clap hands.)*
>
> With hands, say "I love you!"
> *(Hug one another.)*

© 1992 Tabor Publishing
Permission to duplicate is granted.

PART ONE
Using Our Hands

Read with Me

Look at your hands. Wiggle your fingers.
Give yourself a hug!
Give a friend a great big hug!

Look at all the things we can do with our hands!

Hands are for <u>helping</u>.

Hands are for <u>eating</u>.

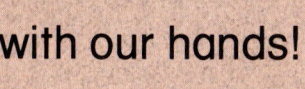

Hands are for <u>loving</u>.

Hands are for <u>playing</u>.

Hands are for <u>working</u>.

Mark what you can do.
Tell a story about one of the pictures.

"Please Give Me a Hand"

It was a sunny fall day at Grandpa Morley's farm. Tommy and his sister, Julia, watched Gramps hard at work, fixing all the loose boards in the pasture fence.

"Say, you two!" Gramps shouted. "Come over here and give me a hand, will you?"

"Sure, Gramps," answered Tommy. "Sure, we'll help you. But what can <u>we</u> do?"

"Look here, now," said Gramps. "Julia, you grab hold of this board, right here. And Tommy, you help me hold this end in place. Then I'll be able to pound the nail right where it has to be!"

The children held on tight, and sure enough, it worked! With a few pounds of the hammer, the nail was in place. It wasn't long before all the loose boards on the fence were fixed.

Tommy and Julia could hardly wait to tell Gran about giving Gramps a hand.

No one else in the whole world
has hands just like yours!
Each hand is different.
Each hand is special.

Draw the outline of your hand
in this space.
Tell us about a time
when you gave someone a helping hand.

We can help others with our hands when we work.
We can help others with our hands when we play.
How are these children using their hands?

Tell us what you will do today
to give someone a helping hand.

Thank God in your heart
for your wonderful helping hands.

Let Us Pray

Catechist: Let us begin with our naming prayer.
All: In the name of the Father,
and of the Son,
and of the Holy Spirit. Amen.
All sing: Alleluia! Alleluia!
Catechist: A reading from the gospel:
Jesus blessed them and said,
"For I was hungry, and you gave Me food.
I was thirsty, and you gave Me a drink."
(From Matthew 25:35)
The gospel of the Lord.
All: Praise to you, Lord Jesus Christ.
Catechist: For those who use their hands
to bring food to the hungry . . .
For those who use their hands
to care for the sick . . .
For those who use their hands
to help people find homes . . .
Let us offer one another a sign of peace.
Let us go in peace to love and serve
the Lord with our helping hands.
All: Thanks be to God. Amen.

PART TWO
Jesus' Helping Hands

Read with Me

Tell how these hands help us. What is your favorite way to help with your hands?

There are many stories in the Bible about how Jesus helped people. Jesus shows us how to use our hands to help one another.

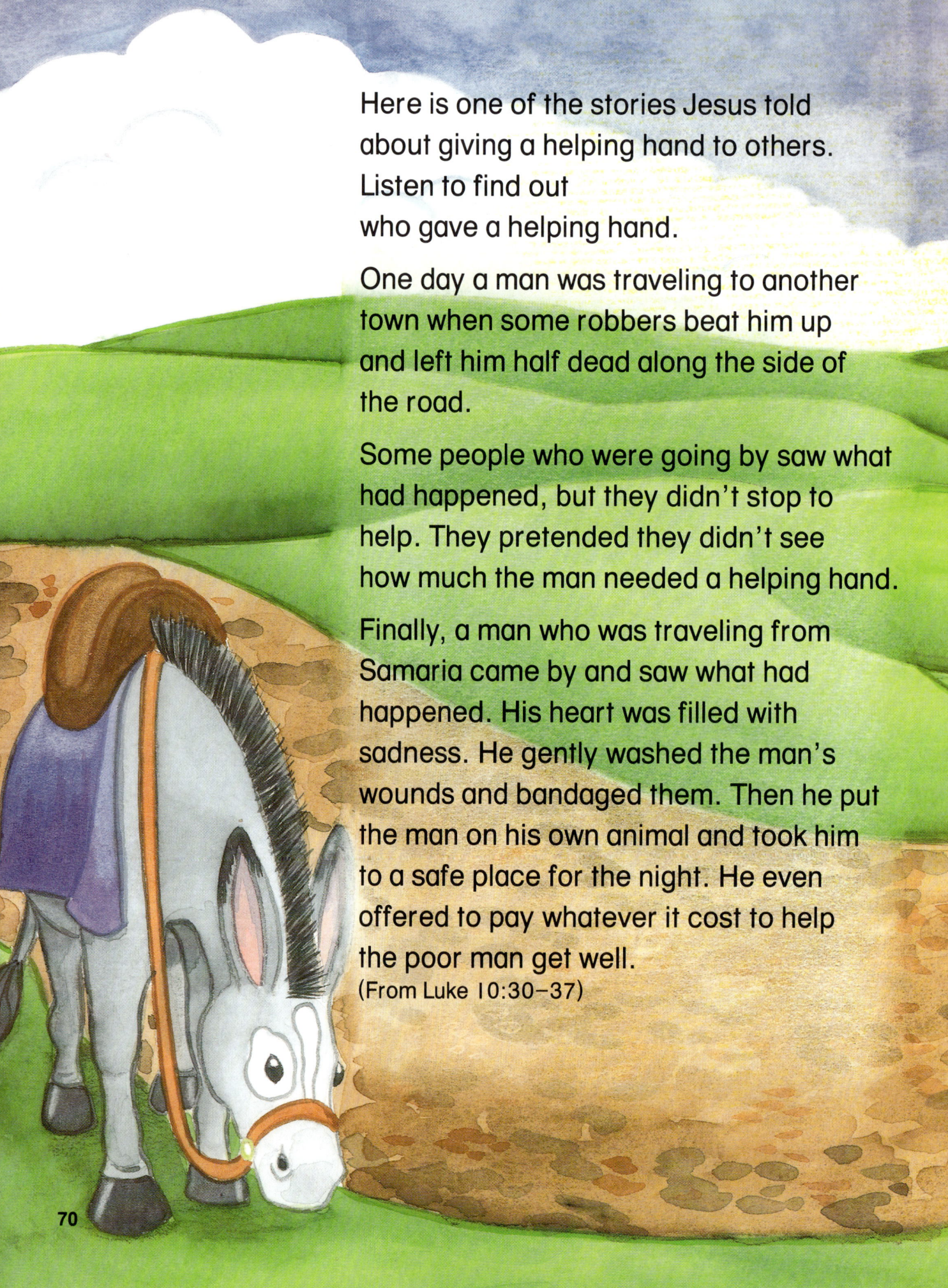

Here is one of the stories Jesus told about giving a helping hand to others. Listen to find out
who gave a helping hand.

One day a man was traveling to another town when some robbers beat him up and left him half dead along the side of the road.

Some people who were going by saw what had happened, but they didn't stop to help. They pretended they didn't see how much the man needed a helping hand.

Finally, a man who was traveling from Samaria came by and saw what had happened. His heart was filled with sadness. He gently washed the man's wounds and bandaged them. Then he put the man on his own animal and took him to a safe place for the night. He even offered to pay whatever it cost to help the poor man get well.
(From Luke 10:30–37)

Then Jesus asked His friends, "Who acted like a good neighbor to the man who was beaten?"

How would you have answered Jesus' question? Can you imagine why Jesus told this story?

Jesus always gave people a helping hand. He wants us to help others, too.

Listen to find out another way Jesus' hands helped people.

One day Jesus and His friends took a long walk together. They walked along a dusty path, for there were no roads or sidewalks in their land. At the end of the day, they all were tired and dirty.

Jesus and His friends were resting after their walk. Jesus got up, tied a towel around His waist, and poured some water from a pitcher into a basin. Then Jesus went from one friend to the next, washed their dusty feet, and dried them with the towel.

Jesus told His friends, "I have given you an example, so that you will do for others just what I have done for you."
(From John 13:4–17)

How did Jesus give His friends a helping hand?
How do you think Jesus wants us to use our hands?

Here are some people who have helping hands. Tell us what is happening in each picture. How are the people doing what Jesus wants us to do?

Draw how you will be a helping hand to someone.

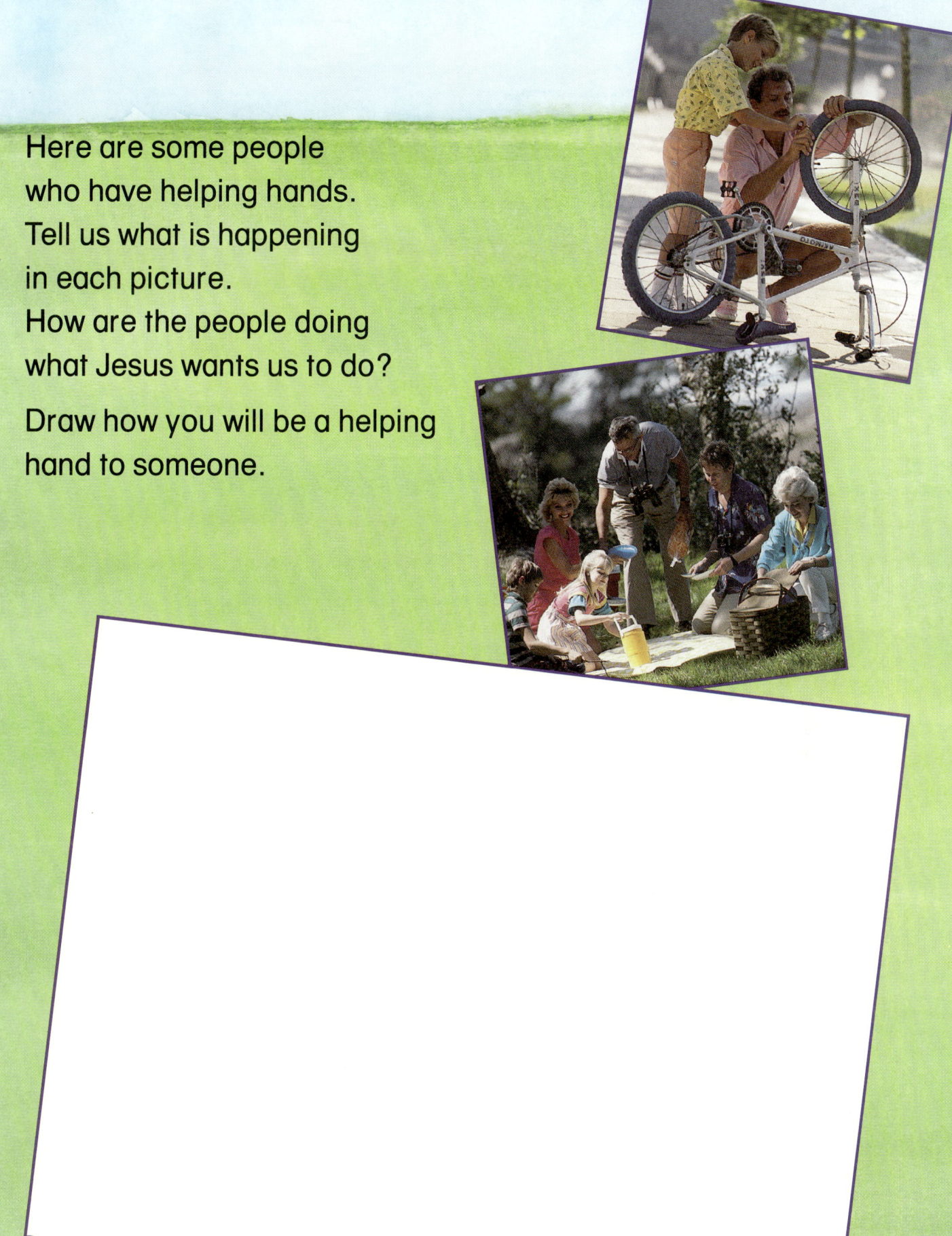

Let Us Pray

Catechist: Let us begin with our naming prayer.
All: In the name of the Father,
and of the Son,
and of the Holy Spirit. Amen.
Catechist: Please stand as we listen to a story
from the Holy Bible.
All sing: Alleluia! Alleluia!
Catechist: A reading from the gospel (page 72).
The gospel of the Lord.
All: Praise to you, Lord Jesus Christ.
Catechist: For people who give a helping hand
to one another . . .
For good neighbors who give us
a helping hand . . .
For showing us how to serve one another
with our hands . . .
Let us go to love and serve
as Jesus did.
All: Thanks be to God. Amen.

PART THREE
Hands That Help Others

Read with Me

How do you think this child feels?
Circle the helping hands.
Tell why these hands are helping hands.

Has anything like this ever happened to you?
Who helps you feel better when you are sick?
Christians bring God's love and care to others with their helping hands.

Francis of Assisi

Here is a story about a special Christian named Francis, who lived a long time ago. Listen to find out how Francis' helping hands brought God's love to many people.

Francis grew up in a small town in Italy called Assisi. His family was rich. They gave Francis everything a young man could want. Francis was spoiled and thought only of himself. He hardly noticed what other people needed or how they felt.

Then, one day, Francis met a sick man. The sick man said, "Help me in the name of Jesus." Francis did not like being near sick people, but he washed the man and bandaged his sores.

From that day on, Francis did all that he could for people who were sick or poor. He treated everyone the way Jesus wants us to do. Francis' helping hands brought God's love to everyone he met.

How did Saint Francis use his hands to bring God's love?

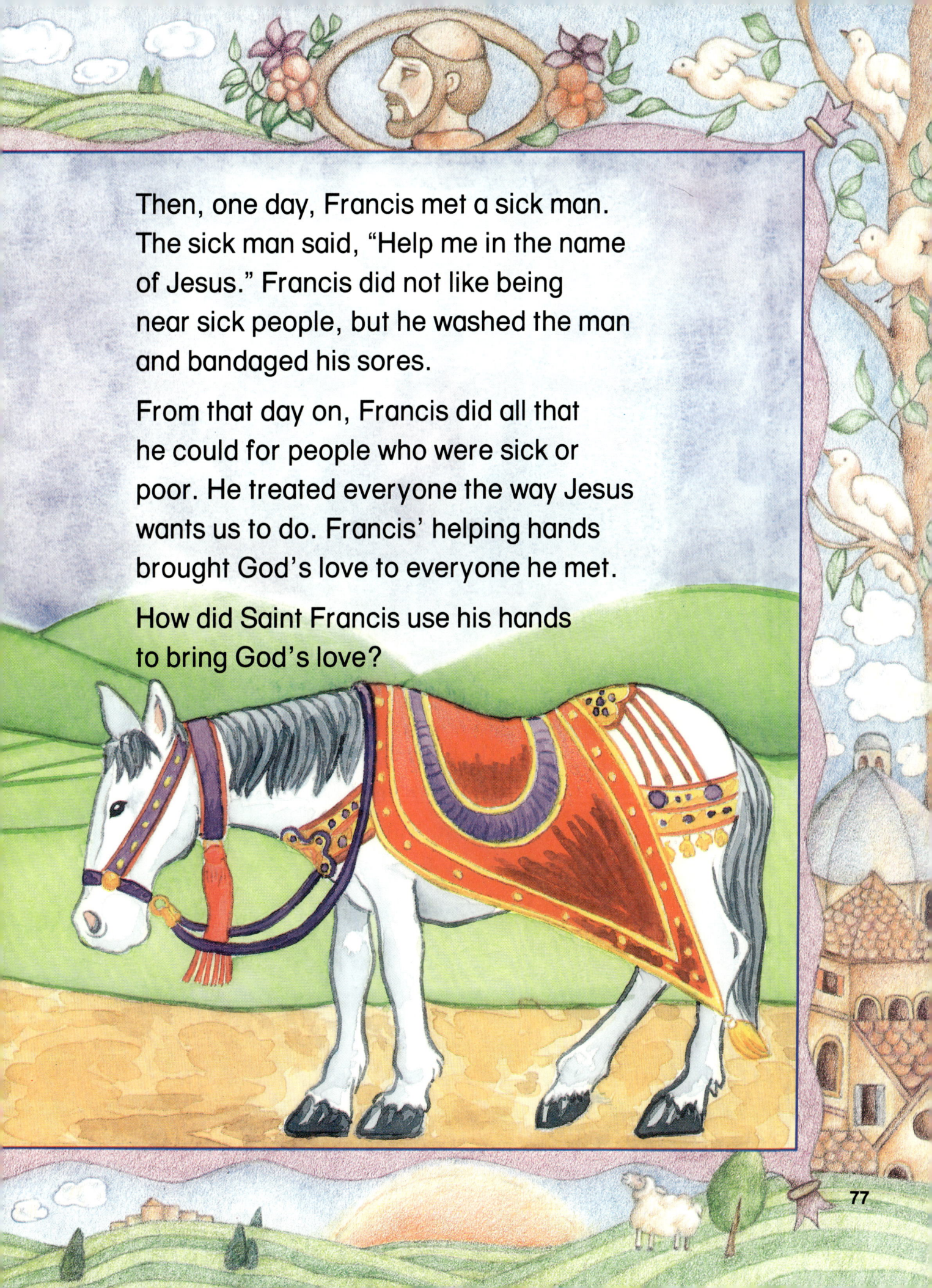

Louise de Marillac

A long time ago, a girl named Louise grew up in France. Her family was very rich and saw to it that Louise had the best of everything. Even though she had everything she wanted, Louise was often sick when she was a child.

When Louise grew up, she saw that many sick people had no one to care for them. She invited other women to help her, and together they started many hospitals and homes for children who had no families.

Many women began to help Louise. They were called the Daughters of Charity because they were so good to the sick. Their helping hands brought healing to many people.

Have you ever helped take care of someone who was sick? How did you use your helping hands to make that person feel better?

Think of a time when you were sick
or you fell and hurt yourself.
Draw a picture to show whose hands
helped you get better.
Tell the story of your drawing.

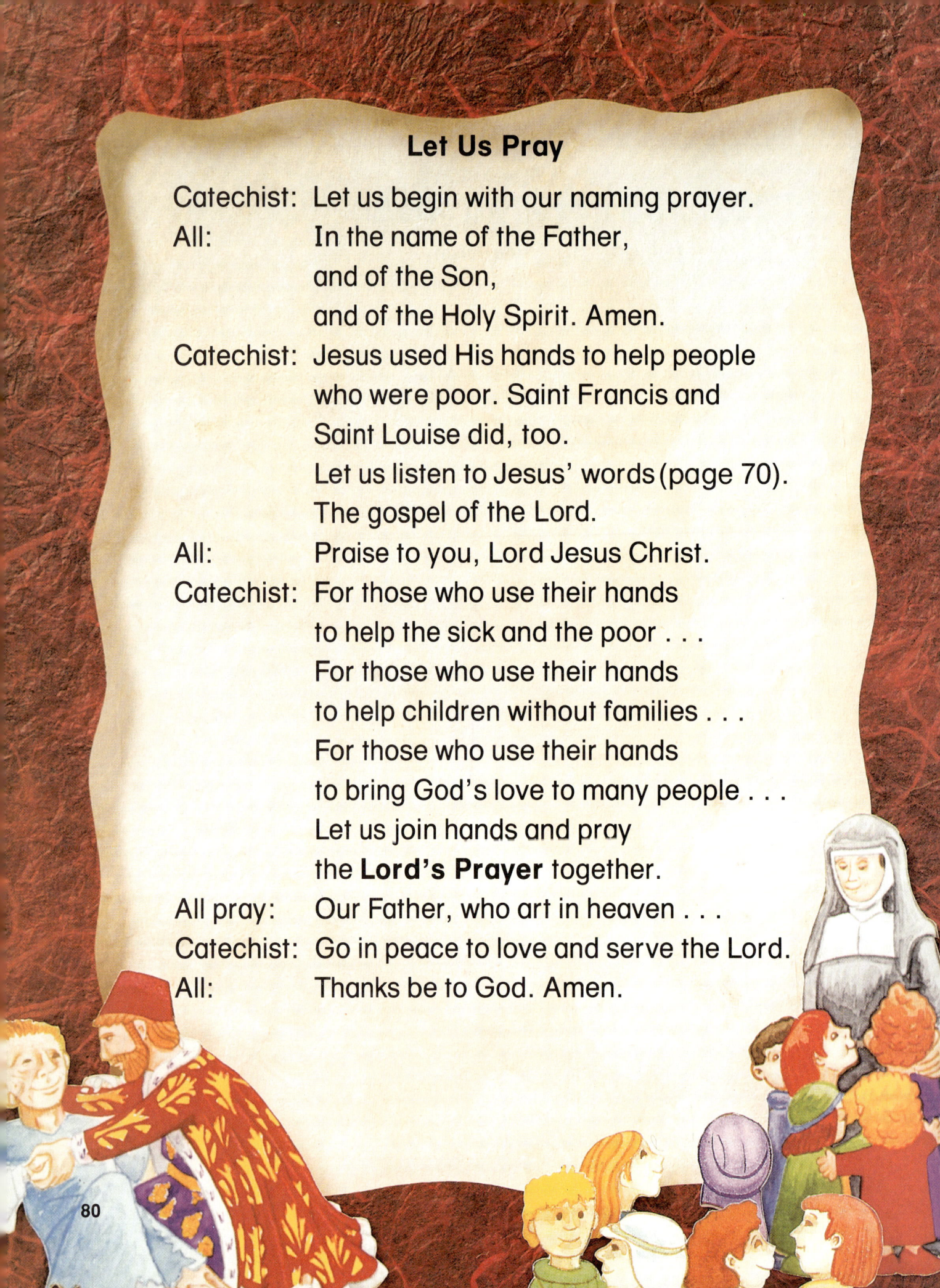

Let Us Pray

Catechist: Let us begin with our naming prayer.
All: In the name of the Father,
and of the Son,
and of the Holy Spirit. Amen.
Catechist: Jesus used His hands to help people
who were poor. Saint Francis and
Saint Louise did, too.
Let us listen to Jesus' words (page 70).
The gospel of the Lord.
All: Praise to you, Lord Jesus Christ.
Catechist: For those who use their hands
to help the sick and the poor . . .
For those who use their hands
to help children without families . . .
For those who use their hands
to bring God's love to many people . . .
Let us join hands and pray
the **Lord's Prayer** together.
All pray: Our Father, who art in heaven . . .
Catechist: Go in peace to love and serve the Lord.
All: Thanks be to God. Amen.

PART FOUR
We Pray with Our Hands

Read with Me

These people are "talking"
with their hands.
What do you think they are saying?

Some people cannot hear well,
and some people cannot hear at all.
Because they cannot hear,
we can "talk" to them with our hands.
They can "talk" to us with their hands, too.
This is called signing.
Do you know anyone
who knows how to sign?

We can talk with our hands
when we pray to God.
What do you think these people
are saying to God with their hands?

Match the drawings with the words.

1. In the name of the Father,
and of the Son,
and of the Holy Spirit. Amen.

2. Amen.

3. Peace be with you.

4. Alleluia!

At Mass, we see people praying with their hands.
Here are some things you will see them do.

We can pray with our hands
while we are saying the **Lord's Prayer.**

When will you pray the **Lord's Prayer?**
Who will you ask to pray with you?

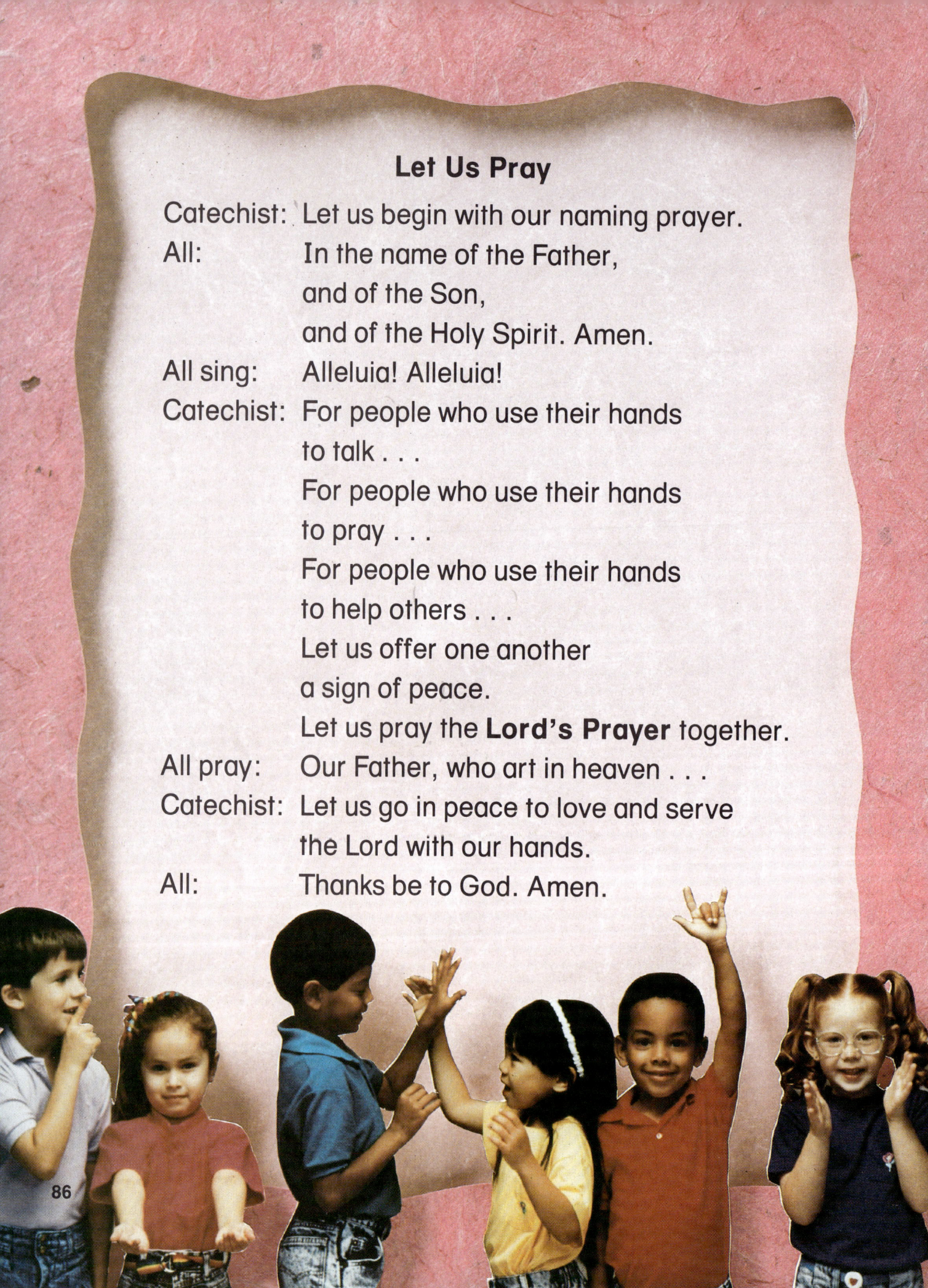

Remembering

Read with Me
Circle the best answer.

1. I can use my hands to help at home. — **YES** / NO
2. I can give a helping hand to other people. — **YES** / NO
3. Some people "talk" with their hands. This is called signing. — **YES** / NO
4. I can use my hands to pray the Lord's Prayer. — **YES** / NO
5. I never use my hands when I play. — YES / **NO**
6. Jesus used His hands to help people. — **YES** / NO
7. Jesus asks us to help others. — **YES** / NO
8. Saint Francis used his hands to wash the sores of a sick man. — **YES** / NO
9. Saint Louise used her hands to help many people who were sick. — **YES** / NO
10. We use our hands to make the Sign of the Cross. — **YES** / NO

Circle the best answer.

1. I feel ___happy___ when I use my hands to help someone.
   sad   (happy)

2. Some people "talk" with their hands because they cannot ___hear___.
   see   (hear)

3. When we use our hands to pray the Sign of the Cross, we say, "In the name of the
   _____,
   Holy Spirit   (Father)
   and of the _____,
   Father   (Son)
   and of the _____.
   Son   (Holy Spirit)

4. Saint Francis and Saint Louise came from _____ families.
   poor   (rich)

5. I feel _____ when I need help and no one gives me a helping hand.
   (sad)   happy

6. _____ hands bring joy to others.
   Clean   (Helping)

4. Ears Are for Hearing

Looking Ahead

Listen carefully! What do you hear? In this chapter we will learn what our ears can do. Have you ever heard stories about Jesus? We will find out what Jesus is telling us in these stories.

Family Matters

Having Ears to Hear

Think back a few years to when your first grader was an infant. Remember how you longed to hear your child speak his or her first words. Recall how, cradled safe in your lap, you spoke softly to your little one: telling stories, sharing secrets, making plans. What were you doing? Talking to yourself? No, never. You were laying the foundation for enrichment.

Now think of a more recent encounter. You crook your finger at your child and say, "Come here." Nothing. No response. You try again, louder. "Hey, listen up! Come here!" Zip. No reaction. You shake your head and wonder if those things hanging on either side of his or her head are anything more than decorations.

These encounters point out two important aspects about having ears to hear. First, most of us communicate through verbal language, which is an imitative act. Hearing your voice, your infant child learned to imitate it and eventually to fashion words on his or her own—to communicate. When we communicate, we do more than transmit and receive information. We shape and name reality. Having ears to hear means, first of all, sharing in inventiveness.

Second, listening really means paying attention. Attentive people know how to attend to—to serve—others. Attending means being responsive, acting compassionately. Having ears to hear also means being aware of and responsive to others.

People of faith—with hearing or without—participate in both aspects of what it means to have ears to hear: They share a world of knowledge, behavior, and belief; they live in that world by being responsive to others and by welcoming others to it. That world is worth hearing about.

Celebrating Ears

Celebrating ears means more than rejoicing in the sense of hearing. It means celebrating our ability to enter, live in, and share the world of faith. Probably the best way to celebrate hearing with children is to tell or read stories. Stories are creative, magical, and world shaping.

Make storytelling part of your regular routine with your child. Share the stories you loved as a child. Allow your child to tell—and read—you the stories he or she enjoys. Communicate with each other; pay attention.

What does having ears to hear mean?

As Catholic Christians, we are a people shaped by the story of Jesus. By hearing that story, paying attention to it, and entering into it, we make it our own and ensure its continuance. Make it your practice to share *the* faith story of each Sunday (the gospel story) with your child, prior to celebrating Mass.

Some evening, prior to Sunday, set your child on your lap—the best seat in the house—and from a children's Bible, read the Sunday gospel. Better yet, tell the gospel story in your own words. Begin by helping your child quiet himself or herself on the inside and the outside. Then share the story. Afterward, conclude with a short prayer that your child can learn by heart.

> Sunday is a listening day,
>   the day Good News is heard.
> Sunday's stories fill us up
>   with God's exciting Word.
> Thank You, God, for Sunday's stories.
>   Amen.

© 1992 Tabor Publishing
Permission to duplicate is granted.

PART ONE
Listening

Read with Me

Which things in these pictures make very loud sounds? Which things make such quiet sounds that you have to listen carefully to hear them?

Try being very still right now. What sounds can you hear? Make a sound like something in one of the pictures. Listen to a friend make a happy sound.

Jared was so excited! The big ✈️ had landed with a ROARRR and he and his mother were in a 🚕 on their way into the big city. Jared's uncle Leon lived in the city, and Jared loved to visit him there.

As they rode along, Jared heard a very loud siren wailing, WHOooo! "I hear a 🚒!" he shouted. "I think it's going to go right by us!" Jared loved the sound of fire engines.

"Here we are," said Mother. She and Jared got out of the taxi and stepped into a tall apartment building. BZZZZZ went the buzzer Mother pushed. Jared listened as Mother pushed the 🔔 again.

"What's that?" Jared asked.

"Uncle Leon will know we're here when he hears that buzzer," Mother answered.

Jared heard the sound of 👞 coming closer, and then the big front door opened.

There was Uncle Leon.

"Hi, Lita. Hi, Jared," Uncle Leon called. Everyone and hugged. The big [elevator] took them up to Uncle Leon's apartment with a **WHIRRR** and soon Jared was happily exploring. So many sounds were coming from the street below that Jared ran to the window to look out.

On one corner, some children were to music. On another corner, there was music coming from an [ice cream truck]

Suddenly Jared heard a little cry coming from a big [basket] on top of Uncle Leon's desk. "What's that?" he asked. Jared carefully lifted the blanket, and the little cry became a great big **RUFFFF!**

"Meet your new [dog]," laughed Uncle Leon.

"Wow! I love him! Thanks, Uncle Leon!" said Jared. "He'll be my best friend!"

Have you ever heard any of these sounds?
What sounds do you like to hear?
What sounds don't you like to hear?

Here is Jared listening at the window.
Imagine that he is listening at a window
in your home.
Draw a picture of some things
that Jared might hear.

Tell us about your drawing.
Make a sound like one of the things
in your drawing.
See if a friend can tell what the sound is.
Then listen to a sound your friend can make.

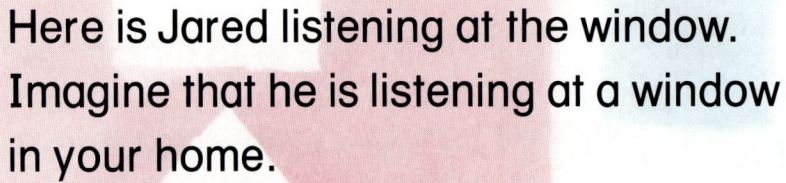

Imagine you can hear
what these people are saying.
What happy words do you hear?
What angry or sad words do you hear?

When we hear sad words, we can show we care.
We can change sad sounds into happy sounds.
Tell about a time when a ☹ sound
became a ☺ sound.

Let Us Pray

Catechist: Let us begin with our naming prayer.
All: In the name of the Father,
and of the Son,
and of the Holy Spirit. Amen.
Catechist: Let us take turns thanking God
for all the sounds we hear in our world.
Child: Thank You, God, for the sound of
_____.
All: Amen.
Catechist: Thank You, God, for giving us our ears
to hear with.
God bless our ears that hear all these
wonderful sounds.
All: Amen.

PART TWO
We Listen to Stories about Jesus

Read with Me

Do you like to listen to stories?
Who is your favorite storyteller?
Is there someone who tells your
family's stories over and over again?
Why do you like to listen
to your family storyteller?

Jesus was a great storyteller.
Many of Jesus' friends
were storytellers, too.
They told stories about Jesus
to the people.
We call Jesus' friends His disciples.

Jesus' disciples wanted all the people to hear about Jesus.
They wanted the people to know all that Jesus said and did.
Listen to this story they told about how Jesus gathered His disciples.

One day Jesus was walking along the shore of Lake Galilee. He saw two brothers, Peter and Andrew, catching fish in the lake with a big net.

Jesus said to them, "Come with Me."

The two fishermen left their nets and went with Jesus.

As Jesus walked along, He saw two other brothers, James and John, out on the lake. They were fishing from their boat with their father.

Jesus called out to them, "Come with Me!" James and John heard Jesus call. They left their boat and their father and went with Jesus. (From Matthew 4:18–22)

Here are some other stories about Jesus that you have heard before.
Listen to them again.

The Woman at the Well
(From the gospel according to John)

Jesus and the Children
(From the gospel according to Luke)

Ask someone in your family to listen while you tell these stories about Jesus. Use these pictures to help you.

Jesus and Zaccheus
(From the gospel according to Luke)

Jesus Washes the Disciples' Feet
(From the gospel according to John)

Let Us Pray

Catechist: Let us begin with our naming prayer.

All: In the name of the Father,
and of the Son,
and of the Holy Spirit. Amen.

Catechist: Let us stand and listen to a special story about Jesus from the gospel of Saint Luke (page 42).

All sing: Alleluia!

Catechist: The gospel of the Lord.

All: Praise to you, Lord Jesus Christ.

Catechist: Let us have a moment of quiet to think about the gospel story we have just heard.

God, bless our ears that listen to Your stories.

All: Amen.

PART THREE
We Listen to Jesus' Teachings

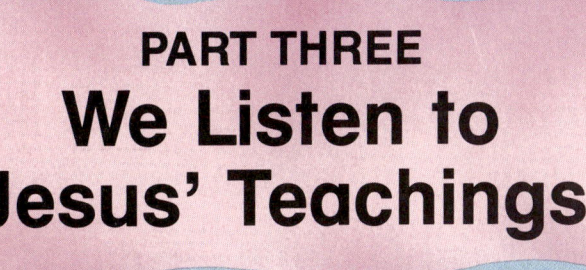

Read with Me

What do you think these friends are saying to each other?

Good friends listen to each other.
We listen at home and at school
and at play.
We listen to people who love us.
We listen to what they teach us.

Who listens to you?
To whom do you listen?
How are you a good listener?

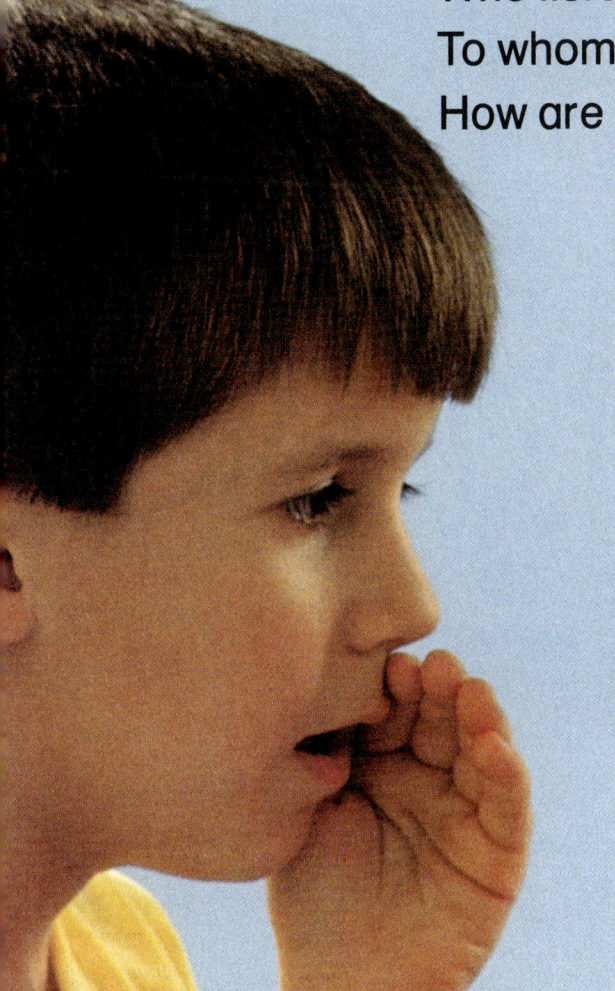
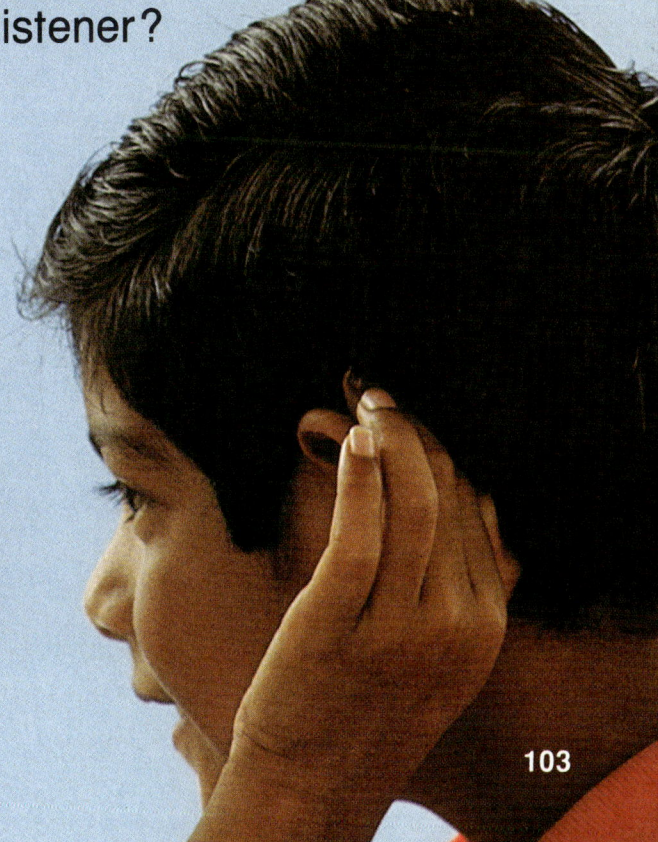

Jesus tells us that He is our friend.
When Jesus was teaching, He said,

"Listen to Me!" (From Mark 4:3)
"You are My friends if you do what I ask you." (From John 15:14)

Friends listen to each other.
We are friends of Jesus.
We listen to Jesus' teachings
when the gospels are read to us
from the Bible.
We listen to learn how Jesus wants us to live.
We try to do what Jesus asks us.

Listen to this story from the gospels.
You will hear another one of Jesus' teachings.

One day a crowd of people were with Jesus on a hillside. The people gathered around Jesus, and He began to teach them. He said,

> "Happy are those who work for peace.
> They are God's children."
> (From Matthew 5:1–2, 9)

How can you work for peace in your family?
How can you be a peacemaker for your friends?

Another day someone asked Jesus,
"How does God want us to live?"
Jesus listened to the question and said,

"Love the Lord your God
with all your heart,
with all your soul,
and with all your mind."
(From Matthew 22:34–37)

Friends of Jesus listen to Him.
We try to live as Jesus teaches us.

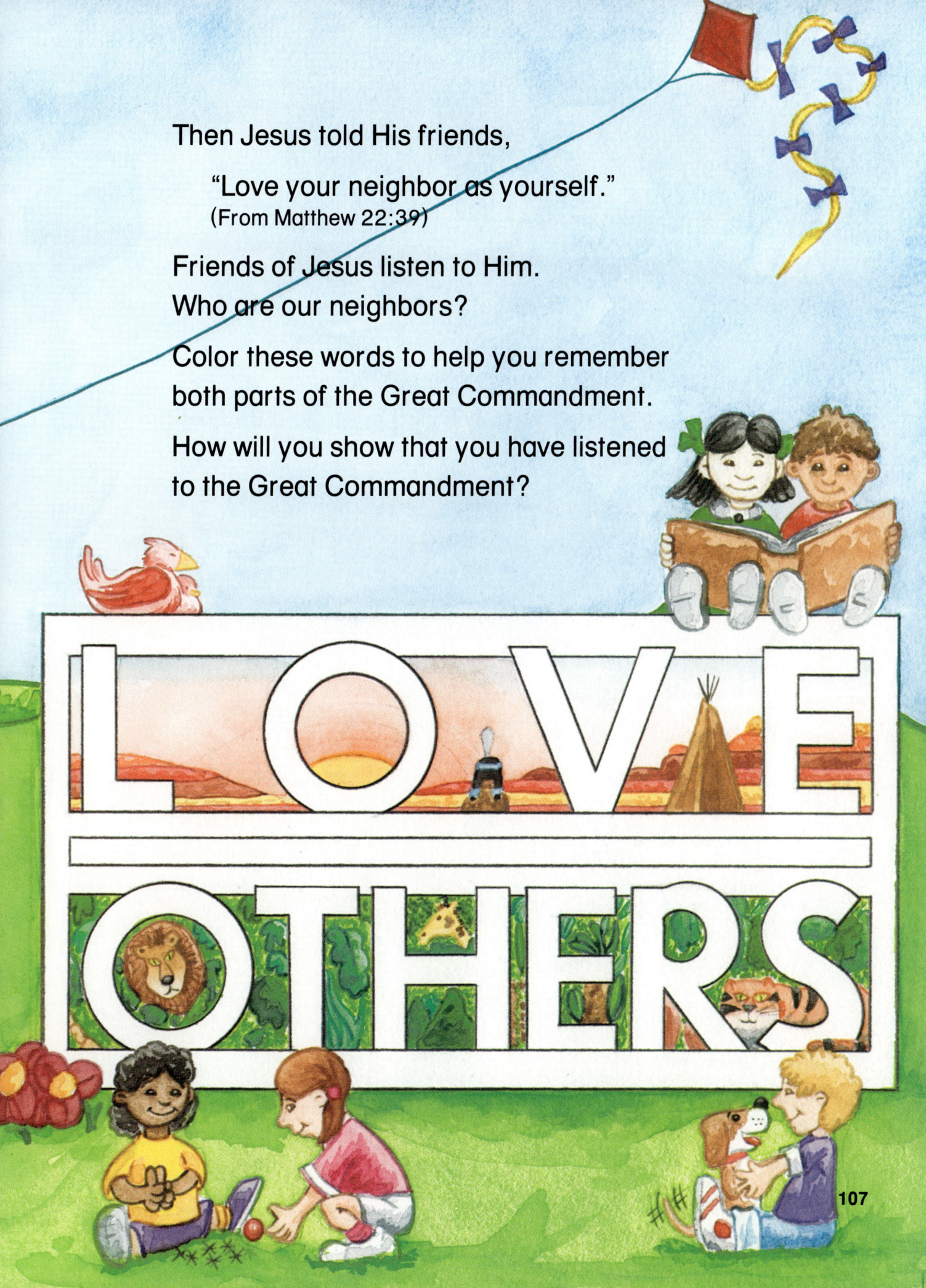

Then Jesus told His friends,

"Love your neighbor as yourself."
(From Matthew 22:39)

Friends of Jesus listen to Him.
Who are our neighbors?

Color these words to help you remember both parts of the Great Commandment.

How will you show that you have listened to the Great Commandment?

LOVE
OTHERS

Let Us Pray

Catechist:	Let us begin with our naming prayer.
All:	In the name of the Father, and of the Son, and of the Holy Spirit. Amen.
Catechist:	Let us stand and listen to what Jesus tells us to do in the gospel of Saint Matthew.
All sing:	Alleluia!
Catechist:	The gospel of the Lord.
All:	Praise to you, Lord Jesus Christ.
Catechist:	Let us have a moment of quiet to think about what we have heard Jesus say. For those who . . . let us pray to the Lord.
All:	Lord, hear our prayer.
Catechist:	God bless our ears that help us to listen to what Jesus does and says in the gospels.
All:	Amen.

PART FOUR
We Listen at Mass

Read with Me

What do you think these people are doing?
Why are the people listening so carefully?

"Happy are those who hear the Word of God and obey it," the lector read.

Maria snapped her head up when she heard the word <u>obey</u>. Most Sundays she was a good listener at Mass. She loved to hear all the stories of Jesus and His friends.

Maria heard the lector say, "This is the Word of the Lord." She joined in saying, "Thanks be to God."

But today Maria was not happy. She was thinking about what had happened before Mass. She had been playing at Bridget's house. Bridget had a board game like Maria's. But Bridget's game was new and still had all the pieces. Maria had lost two markers from her game, and it was not much fun without them. So Maria had slipped two of Bridget's markers into her backpack while Bridget was out of the room. "She won't notice," thought Maria.

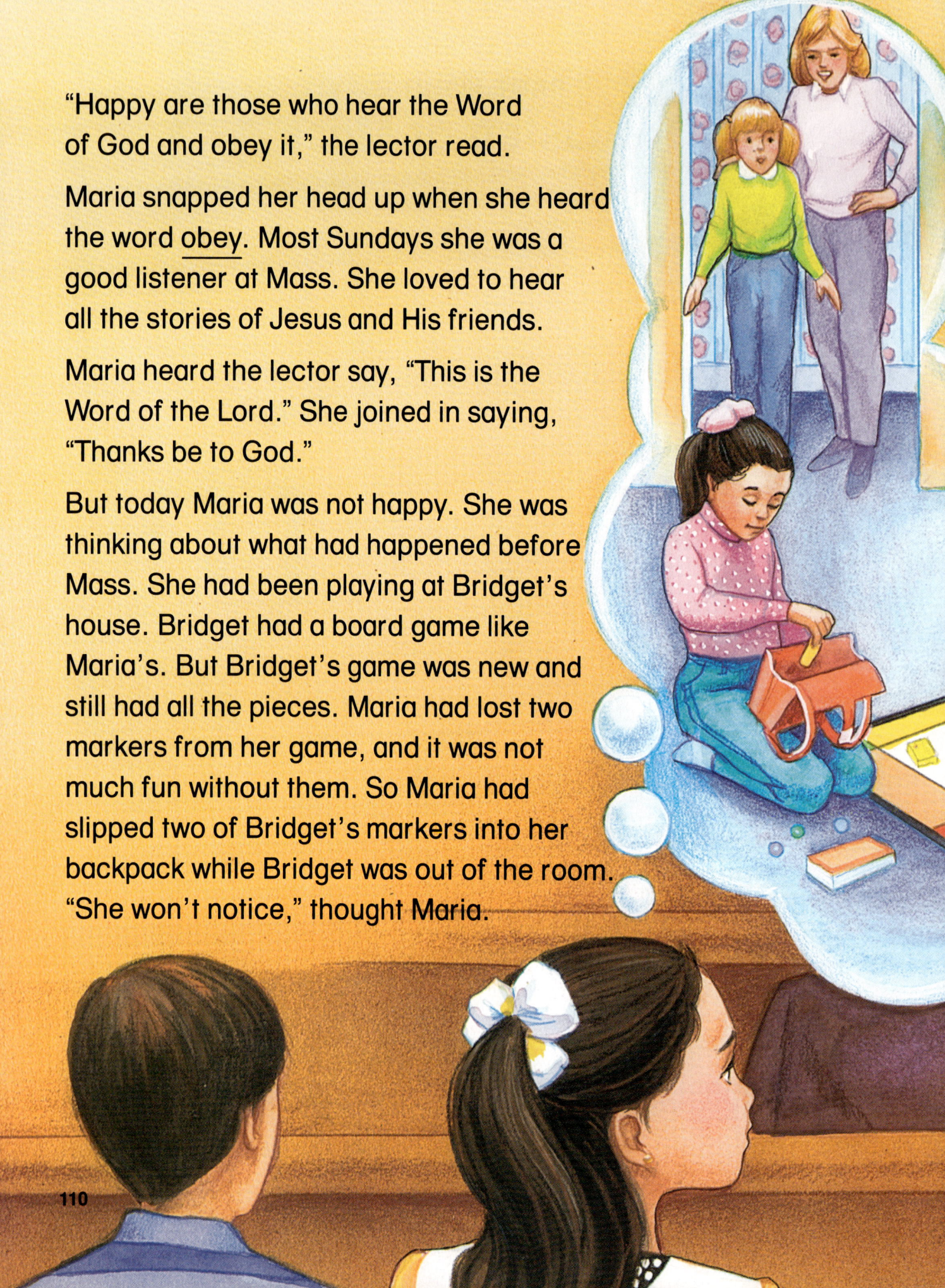

But Bridget had noticed. She had become very upset and so had her mother.

Now, as Maria listened, she heard the word obey ringing in her ears. She remembered her mom's words, "When we hear God's Word and obey it, we are happy."

"Maria, stand up!" she heard now, as her mother looked down at her. Maria quickly stood up with everyone else. She knew it was time to listen to the gospel. She remembered that we stand to show how happy we are to listen to the Good News of Jesus.

The gospel told the story of how Jesus had forgiven someone. "Jesus is such a good friend," thought Maria. "I wasn't a very good friend to Bridget."

After the gospel reading, Father John said, "This is the gospel of the Lord."

Everyone answered, "Praise to you, Lord Jesus Christ." So did Maria. But she did not feel she had lived as Jesus' friend this morning.

Then Maria's parish family prayed for one another and for all the people in the world.

As Maria listened to the prayers, she joined in the response, "Lord, hear our prayer." She knew God listens to us. So quietly, Maria added her own little prayer for Bridget and for Bridget's mother. She asked God to hear her prayer and the prayers of everyone all over the world.

As Mass ended, Maria listened to the songs of the choir. She knew she would go back to Bridget's house. She would simply say, "Bridget, I'm really sorry I took your game markers. I'll never do it again."

Somehow Maria knew that it would be all right. As she heard the church bells chime, she even imagined she could hear herself and Bridget laughing.

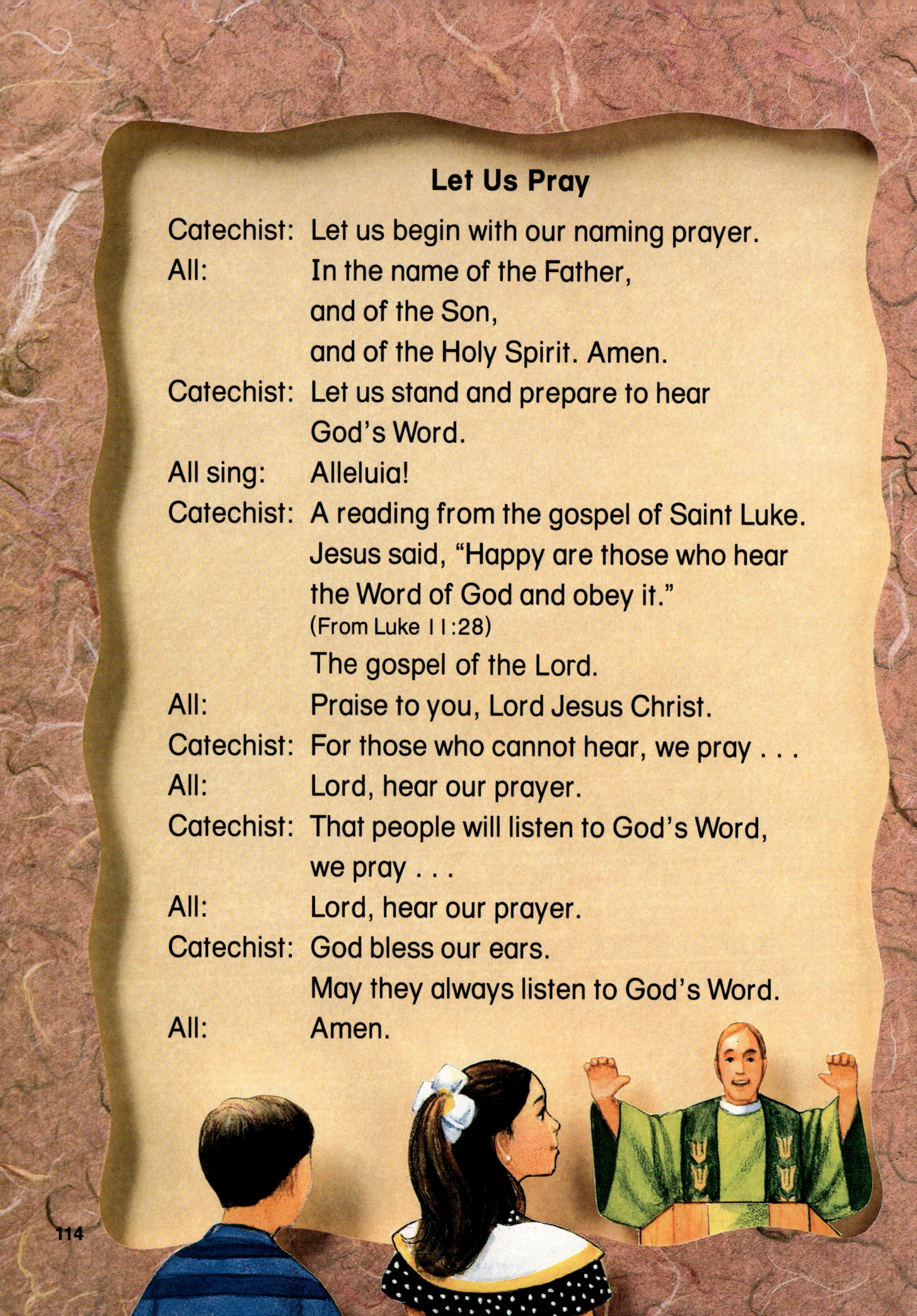

Let Us Pray

Catechist: Let us begin with our naming prayer.
All: In the name of the Father,
and of the Son,
and of the Holy Spirit. Amen.
Catechist: Let us stand and prepare to hear God's Word.
All sing: Alleluia!
Catechist: A reading from the gospel of Saint Luke. Jesus said, "Happy are those who hear the Word of God and obey it."
(From Luke 11:28)
The gospel of the Lord.
All: Praise to you, Lord Jesus Christ.
Catechist: For those who cannot hear, we pray . . .
All: Lord, hear our prayer.
Catechist: That people will listen to God's Word, we pray . . .
All: Lord, hear our prayer.
Catechist: God bless our ears.
May they always listen to God's Word.
All: Amen.

Remembering

Read with Me

Circle the best answer.

1. I try to be a good listener. YES NO

2. I am sad when I listen to people who love me. YES NO

3. Jesus' friends are called His disciples. YES NO

4. Jesus said to His disciples, "Come with Me." YES NO

5. The disciples told stories about Jesus. They wanted the people to know what Jesus said and did. YES NO

6. We listen to Jesus' teachings when the gospels are read to us. YES NO

7. Jesus said, "You are My friends if you do what I ask you." YES NO

8. I know the Great Commandment by heart. YES NO

9. Jesus said, "Happy are those who hear the Word of God and obey it." YES NO

Circle the best answer.

1. Good friends _____ to each other.
   sing   listen

2. Many of Jesus' friends told _____ about Jesus.
   lies   stories

3. Jesus was a great _____.
   hunter   storyteller

4. Jesus tells us that we will be happy when we work for _____.
   money   peace

5. Some of Jesus' friends were _____.
   fishermen   hunters

6. One of Jesus' disciples was named _____.
   John   Michael

7. The Great _____ teaches us how God wants us to live.
   Law   Commandment

8. Jesus told His friends, "Love your _____ as yourself."
   family   neighbor

5. Eyes Are for Seeing

Looking Ahead

How far can you see? Can you see an ant or the moon? In this chapter we will discover what our eyes can do. We cannot see God, but we can see the wonderful things that God has made.

Family Matters

Believing Is Seeing

A parent watched her first grader putting a puzzle together. Such concentration! Such diligence! He grappled with the pieces, laying them this way and that. He would recognize parts of the puzzle's solution (a pony), but then would struggle with their sequence. At last, he wedged the last piece in. What delight shown on his face! What joy! The pony was always there, but it took time and effort to see and recognize it. So it is with God. God is always here, but it takes time and effort to see and to recognize God. Ah, but when we do see and recognize, what delight! What joy!

When it comes to eyes, seeing, and faith, it is important to recall that Jesus seemed to believe in the old saw, "Seeing is believing." Recall how those to whom Jesus gave the gift of seeing lost no time in recognizing that their sight was to be used not just to skim the surface of reality but to dive beneath it and there to discover the really Real, there to see what was worth seeing and worth believing in.

Jesus—Love at first sight!

Picture yourself as a person blind from birth who has just been touched by Jesus. Visualize the rush of form, color, texture, and dimension that would explode upon you. Imagine your immense pleasure as you gaze into Jesus' eyes. What would you be looking at? An ordinary man, bearded and somewhat bedraggled? No, you'd be seeing more than that. You'd be looking at Love at first sight. What delight! What joy!

Such love, delight, and joy do not exist only in our imaginations. They are all around us if we but look and see. In all creation, we can discover the wonders of God. In people especially, we can discover the face of Jesus, who claimed to be identified with and in every human face.

Celebrating Sight

Gazing at a hazel nut, Saint Julian of Norwich asked of God, "What may this be?" She was answered, "It is all that is made.... It lasts and ever shall, because God made it, God loves it, God keepeth it." In this simple observation, Saint Julian demonstrated how seeing is believing and how believing is seeing more than meets the eye.

Celebrate seeing more than meets the eye by encouraging your child to join with you in one or both of the following activities.

- *Seeing in the Squiggle.* Draw a squiggle on a sheet of drawing paper. Ask your child to see if he or she can find an animal or a person "in" the squiggle by drawing in its features.

- *Spyglass Treasure Hunt.* Use paper towel rolls as spyglasses, decorating them with art materials if you wish. Then choose something to look at, such as a large tree. Sit close enough so that only a small portion of the tree can be seen through the spyglass. Have your child focus on a spot and describe what he or she sees. See if you can find the spot with your spyglass. Move closer or farther away and repeat the activity.

Whichever celebration activity you choose to share with your child, conclude by wrapping it in prayer:

> Thank You, God, for things to see:
> For people, earth, and sky.
> Thank You, too, for showing me
> You're more than meets the eye.
> Amen.

Some good books to share with your child about eyes and seeing are *The Eye Book* by Theodore Le Sieg and *Walk with Your Eyes* by Marcia Brown.

PART ONE
What Can We See?

Read with Me

See what is on the computer screen!
What colors can you see on the screen?
What shapes can you see?
Use your crayons to make "animals"
from the shapes.

Sometimes our eyes need help
to see things that are very small.
Here are some things we can use
to help us see better.
Tell what you see in these pictures.
Do you know anyone who uses these things
to see better?
Do you know anyone who cannot see at all?

Sometimes our eyes need help
to see things that are far away.
Here are some things we can use.
Tell what is happening in these pictures.
Do you know anyone who uses these things
to see far away?

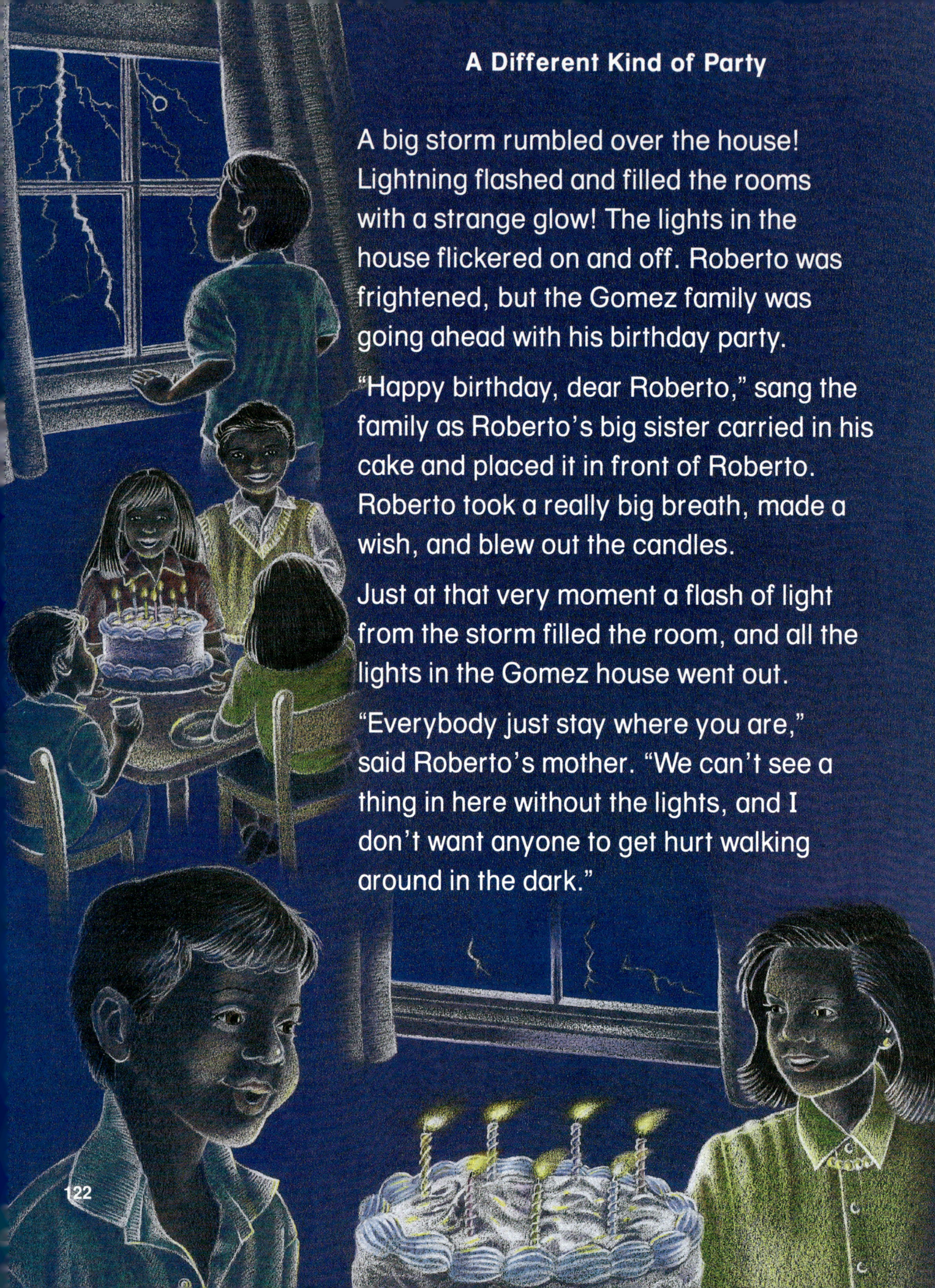

A Different Kind of Party

A big storm rumbled over the house! Lightning flashed and filled the rooms with a strange glow! The lights in the house flickered on and off. Roberto was frightened, but the Gomez family was going ahead with his birthday party.

"Happy birthday, dear Roberto," sang the family as Roberto's big sister carried in his cake and placed it in front of Roberto. Roberto took a really big breath, made a wish, and blew out the candles.

Just at that very moment a flash of light from the storm filled the room, and all the lights in the Gomez house went out.

"Everybody just stay where you are," said Roberto's mother. "We can't see a thing in here without the lights, and I don't want anyone to get hurt walking around in the dark."

Just then more lightning flashed! It filled the kitchen with light again.

"Look at that!" shouted Roberto's sister. "When the lightning flashes, we can see! I know where the matches and some candles are. I'll get them when the lightning flashes again!"

"And I'll get the flashlight that's in the drawer by the sink," said Roberto's big brother. "We don't know how long the lights will be out."

It was the strangest birthday party the family ever had. They ate cake and ice cream, and Roberto opened his presents. But the only light in the house came from the lightning flashes, the candles on the table, and the flashlight. The light changed night into day!

When it is dark, what helps us to see? What things can you do at night because lights help you to see?

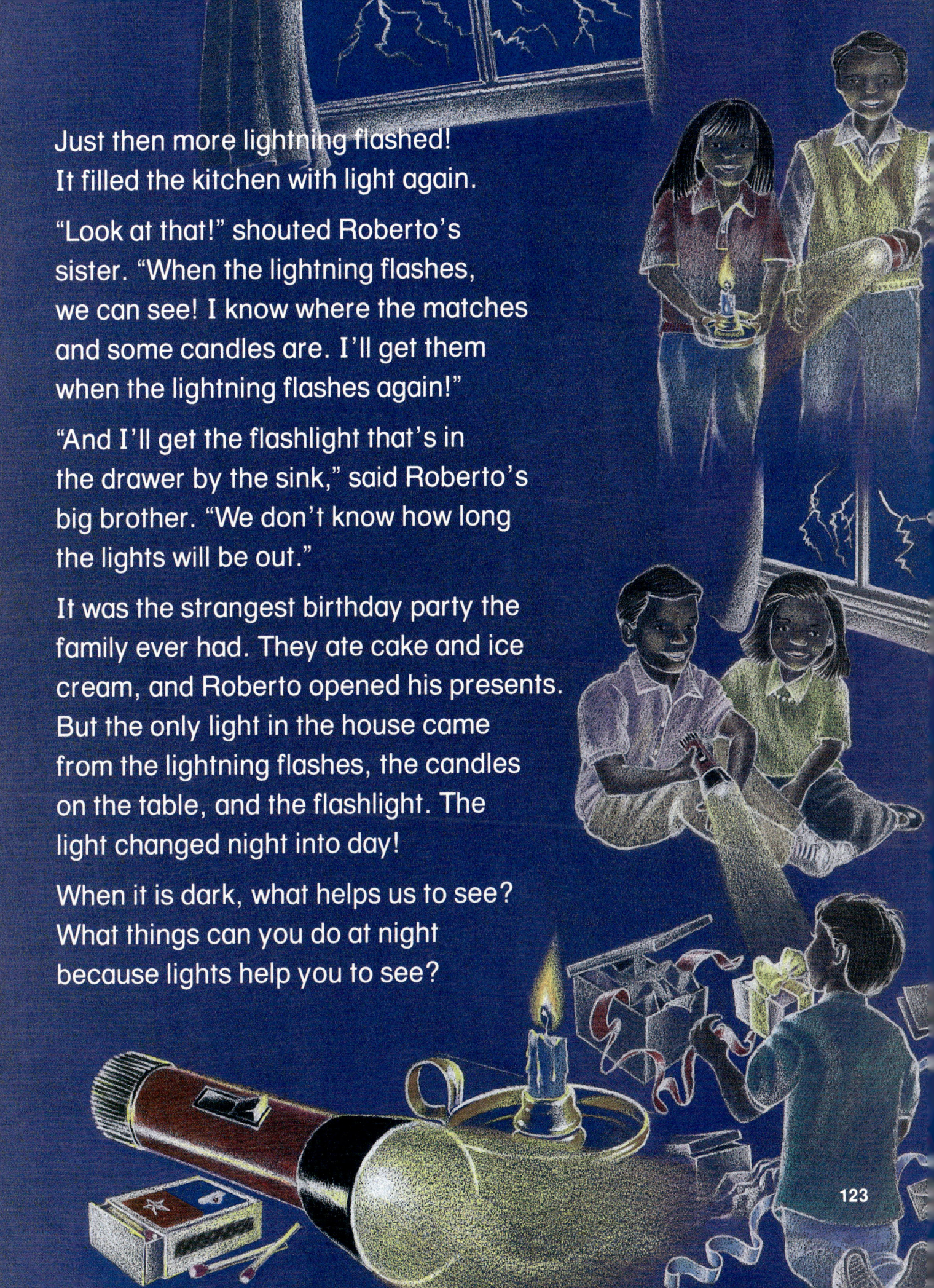

Let Us Pray

Catechist: Let us begin with our naming prayer.
All: In the name of the Father,
and of the Son,
and of the Holy Spirit. Amen.
Catechist: Let us take turns thanking God
for all the wonderful things we can see
with the help of light.
Child: Thank You, God, for _____.
All: Our eyes help us to see.
Catechist: God bless our eyes that see
all these wonderful things.
All: Amen.

PART TWO
We Can See What God Has Made

Read with Me

Our eyes help us see all the wonderful plants and animals in the world.
God made all the plants, animals, stars, and people we see.
Look at the picture on this page.
Color the hidden pictures of things God has made.

Our world is full of wonderful things.
Sometimes we see them.
Sometimes we do not see them.
What do you think this means?

We cannot see God, but we can see
the things that God has made.
The things God made tell us about God.
The things God made praise God.
They show us how wonderful God is.

Can you see the sun today?
Can you see the moon and the stars
from your bedroom window at night?
What else can you see that God has made?

God made all the plants and flowers
and trees.
When we see plants and flowers and trees,
we see what God has made.
All the plants and flowers and trees
show us how wonderful God is.
They give praise to God.
Mark all the growing things you see
in this picture.

What growing things did you see today?
What do they tell you about God?
How can you help to take care of
the growing things in this picture?

We see all the birds and animals God made.
We see all the oceans and rivers God made.
We see the whales and fish God made.
When we see the things that God has made,
we know what God is like.
We know that God is good.

What is your favorite animal?
What river or lake or ocean have you seen?
How can you help to care for the waters
God has made?

When you see all the things God has made, what do you think is the greatest?

Look around you.
What do you see that can walk and talk and think and imagine?

People are the greatest part of God's creation.
People are like God when they take care of everything God made.

Have you seen people taking care of what God has made?
How have you helped them?
How do people praise God?

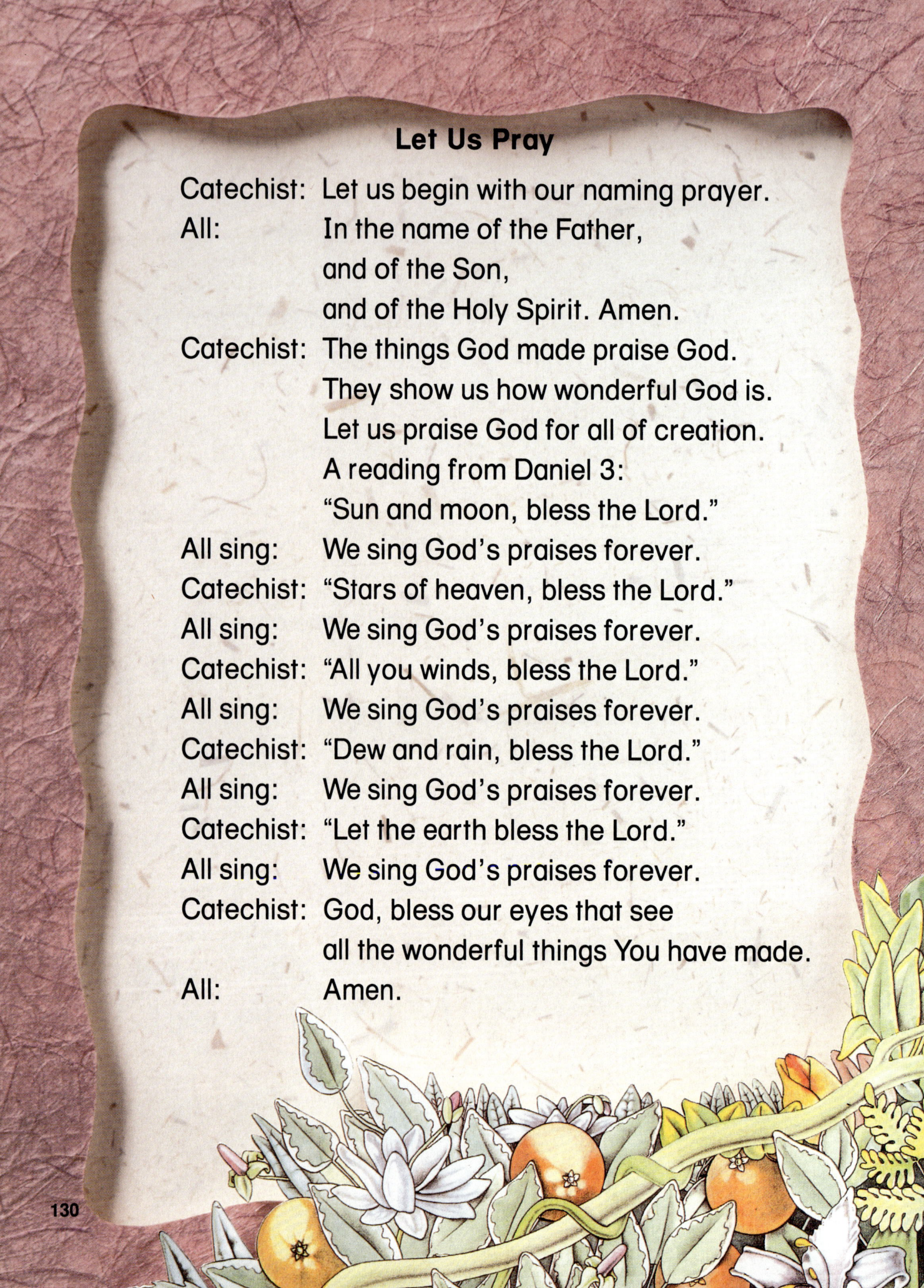

Let Us Pray

Catechist: Let us begin with our naming prayer.
All: In the name of the Father,
and of the Son,
and of the Holy Spirit. Amen.
Catechist: The things God made praise God.
They show us how wonderful God is.
Let us praise God for all of creation.
A reading from Daniel 3:
"Sun and moon, bless the Lord."
All sing: We sing God's praises forever.
Catechist: "Stars of heaven, bless the Lord."
All sing: We sing God's praises forever.
Catechist: "All you winds, bless the Lord."
All sing: We sing God's praises forever.
Catechist: "Dew and rain, bless the Lord."
All sing: We sing God's praises forever.
Catechist: "Let the earth bless the Lord."
All sing: We sing God's praises forever.
Catechist: God, bless our eyes that see
all the wonderful things You have made.
All: Amen.

PART THREE
We Can See the Church

Read with Me

How many people can you see in this picture? All these boys and girls and men and women are like the people who belong to our parish. All these people are the Church. We can see the Church when we see them.

The people we see in our parish are the Church.
We know and love Jesus.
We see the Church when the people in our parish come together for Mass or for a parish picnic.
We see the Church when the people in our parish do good things for others.

Do you see the Church giving food
to families who do not have enough?
Do you see the Church giving clothes
to people who are very poor?
Do you see the Church helping people
who are sick or lonely?
Do you see the Church caring for people
even in faraway places?

What people in our parish do you see serving others in these special ways? Ask someone to help you put the names here.

The Church helps me to
_____
__learn_____ about God.

Our catechist's name is
_____

_____

Our Catechist

The Church helps me to
_____
__pray_____.

Our pastor's name is
_____

_____

Our Pastor

The Church helps me to _hear_ God's Word.

Our lector's name is
_____
_____

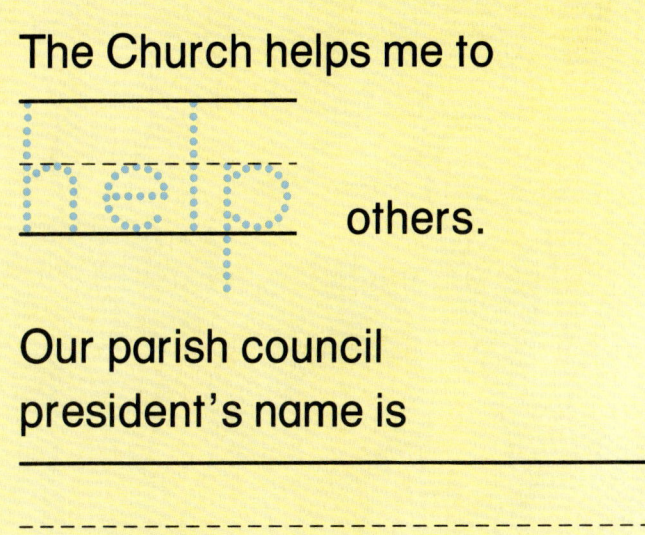
Our Lector

The Church helps me to _help_ others.

Our parish council president's name is
_____
_____

Our Council President

Let Us Pray

Catechist: Let us begin with our naming prayer.
All: In the name of the Father,
and of the Son,
and of the Holy Spirit. Amen.
All sing: We sing God's praises forever.
Catechist: Bless all our friends.
Bless all our families
who love and care for us.
Bless all the people in our parish
who help others.
Bless us as we help others this week.
All: Amen.

PART FOUR
We See Our Parish at Mass

Read with Me

"Hurry, Emily!" called her mother. "We don't want to be late for Mass! Come, let me help you tie your hair ribbon."

Emily was so excited she could hardly stand still. Saint Mark's Church was having a special Mass for the children and their families.

Outside of Saint Mark's Church, Emily saw many families she knew from her block. People called and waved to her family as they walked up the steps in front of the church.

When you go to Mass, who do you see? Do you see people you know?

The people we see at Mass are called the Church.
We all come together to celebrate in the building we call "the church."

Just inside the big church doors, Emily saw Mr. and Mrs. Turlini smiling and welcoming everyone. "The Turlinis are ushers," whispered her mother. "They're going to help us to our seats."

After she was seated, Emily saw her dad's friend, Mr. Lang, standing at the microphone. She knew he was the cantor. "Please join us in singing hymn number 20," he announced. Everyone joined the choir in singing.

When Mass began, Emily watched the procession. She saw Mr. Williams carrying the cross. Some altar servers she knew were in the procession, too. Mrs. Collins was carrying the Lectionary, which would be read during Mass.

As Emily watched and listened to the next part of the Mass, men and women lectors read from the Bible and led the prayers. Then Father Gerald read from the gospels and talked about Jesus.

When you go to Mass,
what do you see the ushers doing?

Do you see boys and girls you know
in the entrance procession?

At Mass, we see many people
helping us to pray.
We see the people in the choir
singing prayers for us.
Do you know anyone who sings
in our parish choir?

Then Emily saw Father Gerald walk over and stand near the altar. She watched to see what he would do next. She saw Father Gerald receiving the gifts of bread and wine. Then he held his arms out to pray. He said a long prayer over the bread and wine. Emily joined hands with her family and prayed the **Lord's Prayer** with everyone.

Next, Emily saw Father Gerald sharing the greeting of peace with the other people around the altar. She shared the greeting of peace with her family and the others around her, too.

Soon Emily saw people coming forward to receive the bread and wine from the priest and from the men and women of the parish. She saw them hold up the bread and say, "The body of Christ."

The people answered, "Amen."

"Soon you will be able to receive Holy Communion, Emily," whispered Dad.

When Mass was over, Emily saw Father Gerald coming back down the aisle in the procession. He joined everyone in singing the last hymn. As she and her family left the church, Emily saw all the happy faces of her friends and neighbors. How proud she was to belong to Saint Mark's parish.

What do you like best about belonging to our parish?

Think about the priest you see at Mass. What is his name?
Draw a picture of him here.

Let Us Pray

Catechist: Let us begin with our naming prayer.
All: In the name of the Father,
and of the Son,
and of the Holy Spirit. Amen.
All sing: Alleluia!
Catechist: For all the people who welcome us to church …
All sing: We sing God's praises forever.
Catechist: For all the people who read to us from the Bible …
All sing: We sing God's praises forever.
Catechist: For all the people who give Holy Communion …
All sing: We sing God's praises forever.
Catechist: For all the people who sing at Mass …
All sing: We sing God's praises forever.
Catechist: For the priest who prays with us …
All sing: We sing God's praises forever.
Catechist: Amen!

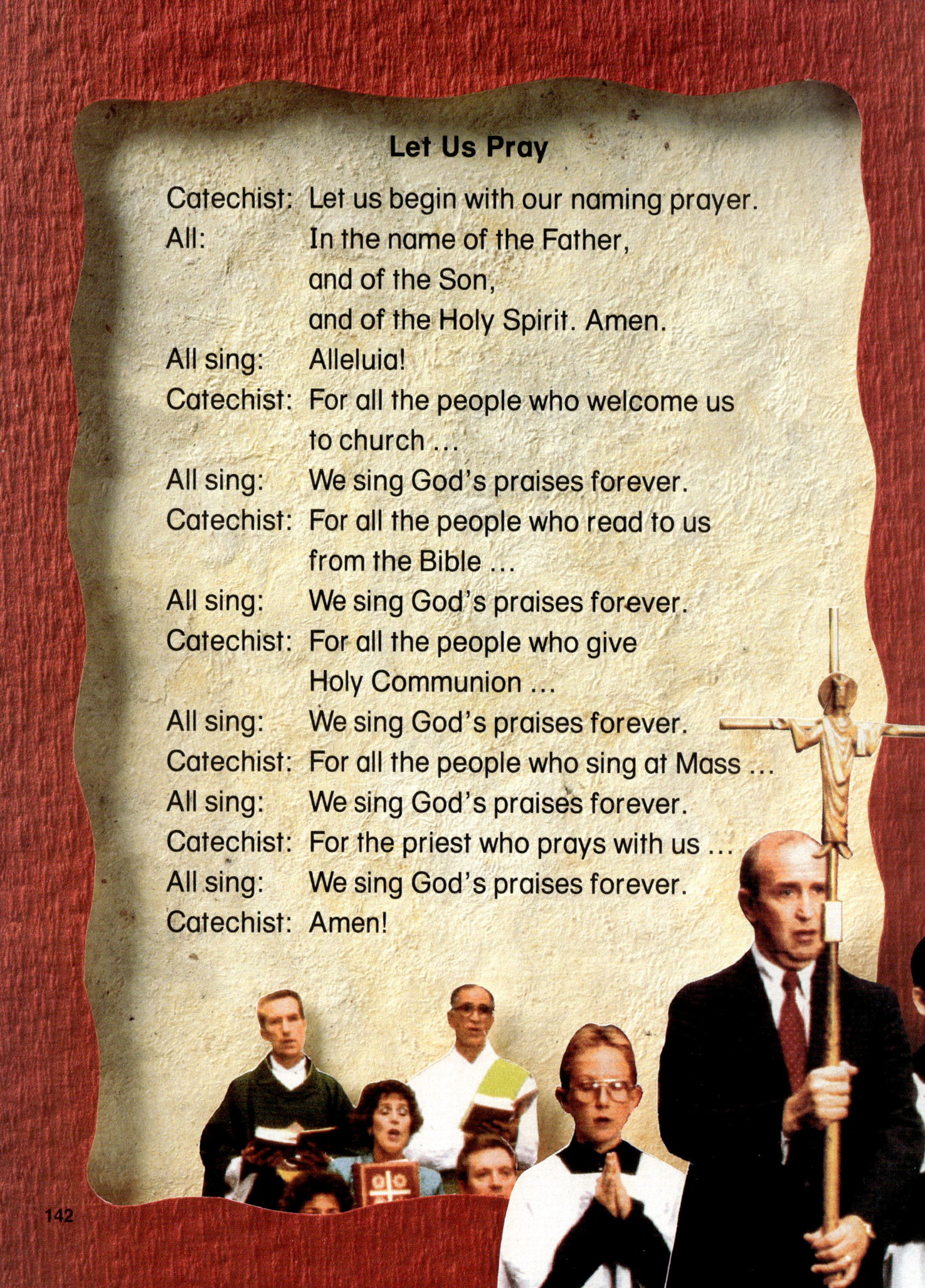

Remembering

Read with Me

Circle the best answer.

1. Some people use eyeglasses to help them see. — YES   NO
2. People do not need light to see. — YES   NO
3. We can see God. — YES   NO
4. We can see God's creation. — YES   NO
5. When I see the beautiful things God has made, I feel sad. — YES   NO
6. All the things God has made give praise to God. — YES   NO
7. The greatest thing God made is the sun. — YES   NO
8. People are the Church. — YES   NO
9. We can see the Church helping people in need. — YES   NO
10. At Mass, we see many people helping us to pray. — YES   NO

Circle the best answer.

1. When I see everything that God has created, I want to say _____ to God.
    "Thank You"   "I'm sad"

2. When it is dark, I cannot _____.
    listen   see

3. People are like God when they take care of _____.
    themselves   God's creation

4. When we see all the things God has made, we know how _____ God is.
    wonderful   busy

5. The things God made tell us about _____.
    creation   God

6. The people we see in our parish are the _____.
    Church   choir

7. At Mass, lectors read from the Bible and lead the _____.
    singing   prayers

8. After we hear "The body of Christ," we say _____.
    "Amen"   the Lord's Prayer

6. Life Is Good

Looking Ahead

Life is a wonderful gift! In this chapter we will discover who gave us life. Do you think that Jesus loved life? Did He work and play and have fun as we do? We will learn how to praise and thank God for life.

Family Matters

Being Alive

When asked to explain how God creates people, a three-year-old girl once shared some unique insight into the meaning of creation and the essence of life.

"See, Daddy, firstest, God takes some dust and mud, squishes them all around, and then puts the bony things in. Then God pushes it all into a lump and wraps skin around it."

Knowing too much, understanding too little, the amused dad said, "Oh, so that's how God makes us and gives us life?"

The little girl shook her curly head. "Unh-uh! Nextest, God puts the lump in secret fire, and *then* we come alive."

That toddler revealed something so simple and fundamental to our understanding of life that we tend to miss it. Namely, everything comes alive and continues to live because of God's "secret fire"—because of God's love.

God's "secret fire" gives us life!

In the chapter "Being Special," you recalled how God made all life out of love and called it "good," with no strings attached. The chapter "Life Is Good" urges your child to show respect for the life God has made and to support it, protect it, and love it in the same way that God does.

Jesus made it clear that love is the electricity of life. He revealed that only those who are loved can love, that God loves us first, and that God's love gives our hearts the trust to love even when love seems impossible.

As parents, you shared in God's vitalizing love when you "loved your child into life." Now it is your job and your joy to fan into full blaze the embers of God's "secret fire" that burns in your child.

Celebrating Life

Over the next few weeks and on into the summer, seize opportunities to celebrate life with your child.

- Encourage your child to use the morning and evening prayers found in Part Four, "Praise God for Life." Each centers on celebrating life.

- Plan and plant a garden together. If you have space in your yard for a garden, wonderful! If not, you can plant one in a space as small as an egg carton. Simply punch small drainage holes in each compartment. Fill the compartments with soil. Plant seeds (use the lid to label them) and add water and sunlight. With a simple prayer, ask God to bless your garden:

   Bless my garden, Lord, I pray.
   Help it grow both night and day.

- Show your child how to make a simple puppet (an old sock with button or drawn-on eyes or a paper plate attached to a flat stick). For instance, your child could make a puppet of a pet he or she takes care of.

   Have your child give the puppet a name. Each night, invite your child to use the puppet to tell his or her own real-life stories about caring for living things.

Helping your child recognize the truth of the chapter "Life Is Good" means helping him or her recognize that life is more precious than what we do or make. Recognizing this leads to reverence for all creation, which leads to wisdom, which spills over into wonder. And only the wonder-filled life is worth celebrating.

© 1992 Tabor Publishing
Permission to duplicate is granted.

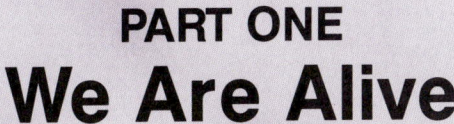

PART ONE
We Are Alive

Read with Me

"When is it ever going to stop raining?" complained Tommy. "I hate it when I can't go out to play!"

Tommy's grandmother smiled to herself. She knew that Tommy was bored. "I have an idea," she said. "Why don't we make your sister's birthday cake now while she is still taking her nap."

Tommy was delighted! He loved cooking with his grandmother. He even liked helping her clean up!

Soon the cake was in the oven and Tommy was helping Gran make the frosting. "Gran," said Tommy thoughtfully, "why do we celebrate birthdays?"

"Because it's so good to be alive," Gran answered. "God gave us a blessing the day you were born. That is something to celebrate!"

What do you think Gran meant?

We can see! We can hear!
We can touch and feel!
We can taste and smell!

Tell us a story about what is happening in each picture.

We are alive! Life is good!

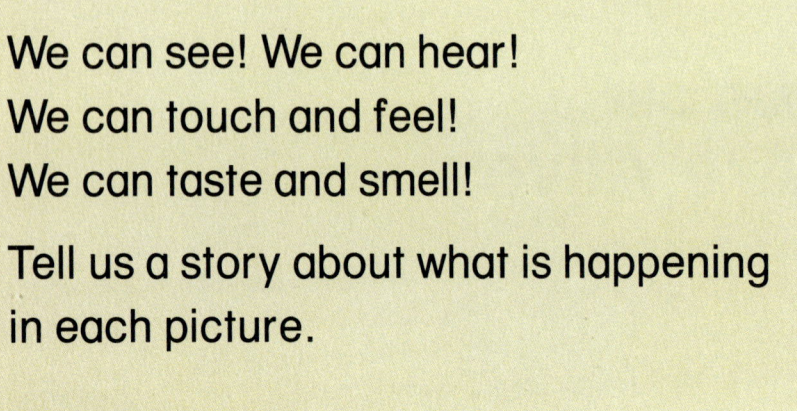

We can walk! We can run and skip!
We can hop and jump and play!

Can you do what is happening in the pictures?

We can think and wonder!
We can remember and imagine!
We can tell stories and learn new things!
We are alive! Life is good!

See What I Can Do!

Mark an X next to all the things you can do.

I can remember—

_____ my phone number.

_____ my address.

_____ my birthday.

I can tell a story about—

_____ my best friend.

_____ the games I like to play.

_____ something funny that happened to me.

I can think and imagine—

_____ what I want to be when I grow up.

_____ how I can help others.

_____ how to play a new game.

We are growing every day!
We are alive! Life is good!
Draw or paste pictures in the spaces
to finish this Growing Chart.

See How I Am Growing

When I was four, I could

When I was five, I could

Now I can

Life is good!

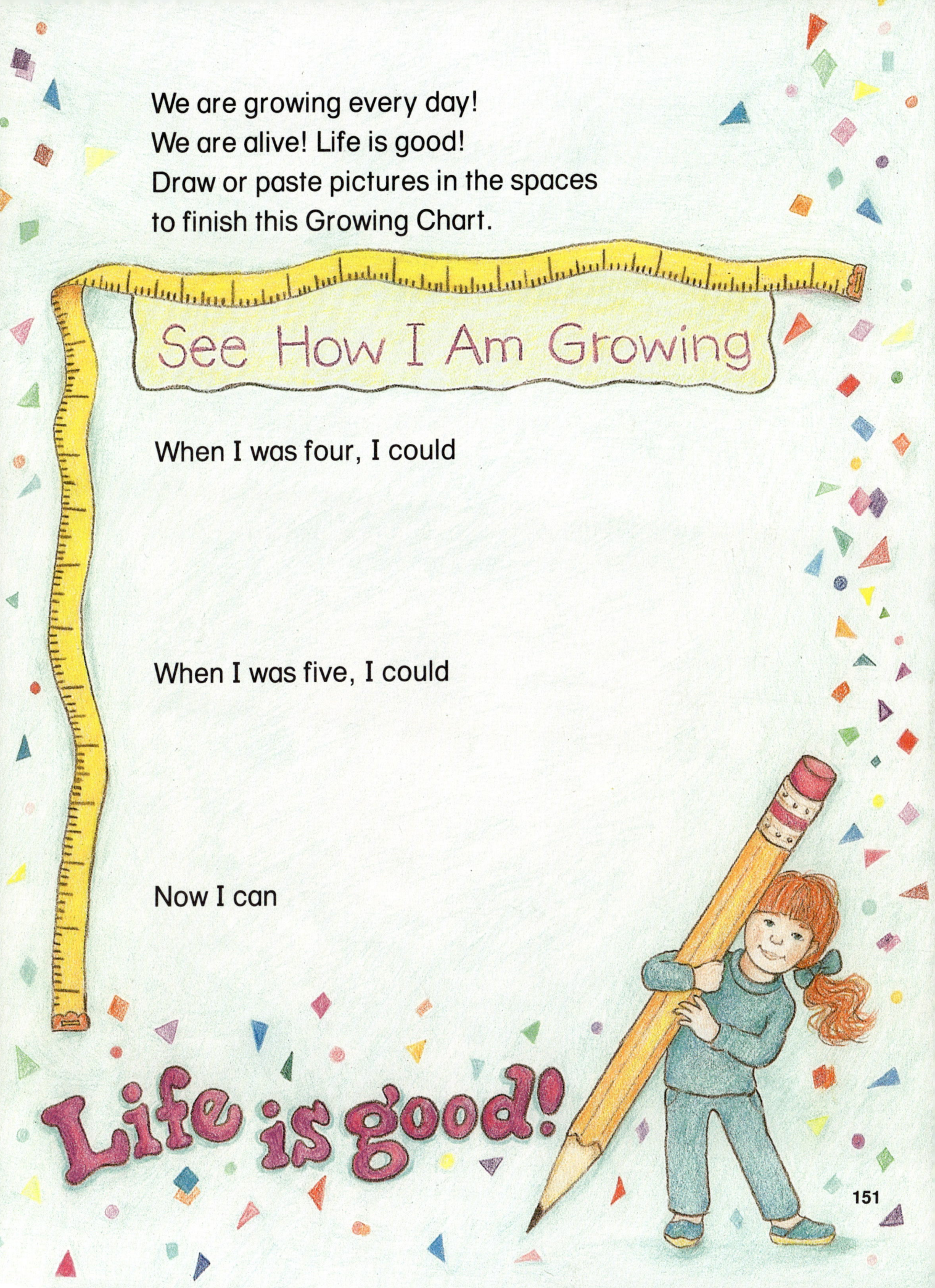

Let Us Pray

Catechist: Let us begin with our naming prayer.

All: In the name of the Father,
and of the Son,
and of the Holy Spirit. Amen.

Catechist: We are thankful for being alive!
Let us use actions to praise God.

Child: Thank You, God, for _____.

All sing: I am wonderfully made! Amen.

PART TWO
God Gives Us Life

Read with Me

Tell us some of the things you can do because you are alive!
Here are some other living things that were made by God.
Tell something you can do that these living things cannot do.

People are the greatest part of God's creation.
People can talk and remember and share with one another.
People can think and make new things.

God gives us the gift of life.

The Bible tells us God said, "Let us make people to be like us." So God created men and women to be in the image of God. (From Genesis 1:26–27)

God created people to be like God. People can love and help one another.

God created people so they could enjoy one another.
God wants us to be happy.
God wants us to enjoy good things.
When do you feel happy?
Who are some of your favorite people?
What things do you like to do best?

God created us to be like God.
We can share God's gift of life
with other people.
We share the gift of life when we
help other people to be happy.
We share the gift of life when we
respect people and what belongs to them.
We share the gift of life when we
treat everyone fairly.
We share the gift of life when we
care for God's creation.

The Bible tells us God said, "Let people be above the fish in the sea, the birds of heaven, the cattle, all wild animals on earth, and all reptiles that crawl upon the earth." (From Genesis 1:26)

God wants people to care for all of creation.

What is your favorite part of God's creation? How do you take care of it?

We all need clean air, water, and land
in order to live.
God gave us these gifts
to make our lives better.
Sometimes people forget and
do not take care of God's creation.
God wants all of us to care for the air,
the water, the trees, and the animals.

Look at the pictures on these pages.
Which ones show people caring for
God's creation?
Check off how you will help.

Let Us Pray

Catechist: Let us begin with our naming prayer.
All: In the name of the Father,
and of the Son,
and of the Holy Spirit. Amen.
All sing: I am wonderfully made! Amen.
Catechist: We have listened to the wonderful story
of creation.
You and I, all of us, are responsible
for the earth and the seas,
the air and the water.
What can we do this week
to take care of our earth?
God, our Creator, help us this week
as we take care of the world
that You gave us.
All: Amen.

PART THREE
Jesus Loved Life

Read with Me

Tell us about one new thing you have learned to do this year.

We are alive! Life is good! Life is a wonderful gift from God.

What is your favorite thing to do?

Jesus enjoyed God's gift of life
when He was growing up.
He liked to do many of the same things
you like to do.

Jesus learned many things from Mary, His mother.

Jesus learned to read and to write.
He learned to make friends and
to be a good friend, too.
He learned to play games with His friends.

Think about some things you like to do.
Do you think Jesus liked to do them, too?
Why or why not?

When Jesus was growing up, He watched
Joseph make things out of wood.
How exciting it must have been
to learn to be a carpenter!
Do you know anyone who is a carpenter?
Jesus learned how wonderful it is
to be alive.
He learned that life is a wonderful gift
from God.

Jesus wants us to be happy.
Jesus tells us that we will be happy
if we show our love for God.

Check some ways you can love God.

What is happening in each picture?
Which things have you done this year?

Jesus tells us we will be happy if we love and help other people.

Who helps you to be happy? How? Who are the people you try to love and serve?

How do you help them to be happy?

Draw how you can make life happier for your family.

Let Us Pray

Catechist: Let us begin with our naming prayer.
All: In the name of the Father,
and of the Son,
and of the Holy Spirit. Amen.
All sing: Alleluia!
I am wonderfully made!
Catechist: Jesus brought happiness to others.
God, bless us and help us
to bring happiness to others, too.
In the name of the Father,
and of the Son,
and of the Holy Spirit.
All: Amen.

PART FOUR
Praise God for Life

Read with Me

How glad we are to be alive!

Draw on the balloons what you like best about being alive.

We praise God for giving us the gift of life.

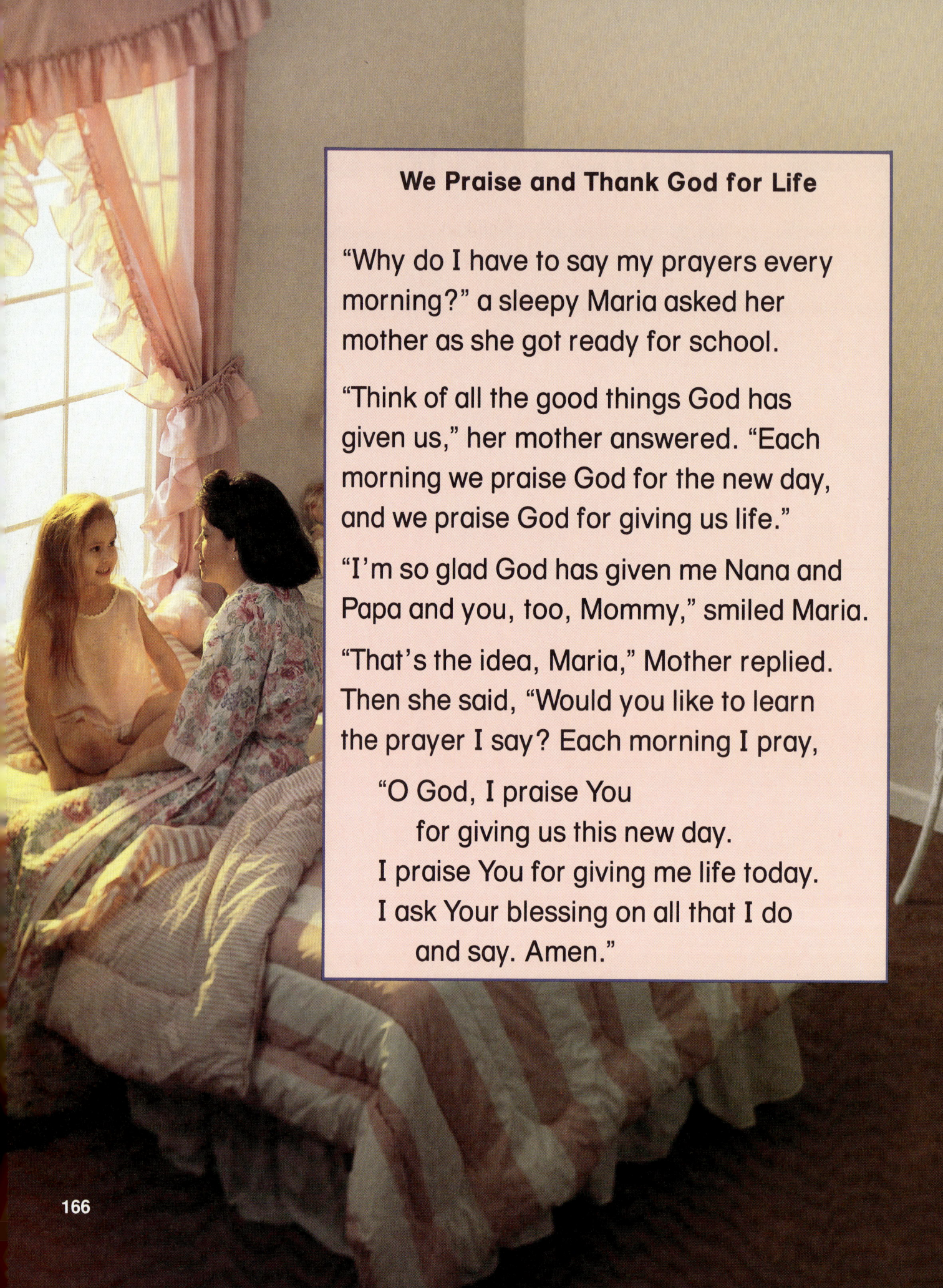

We Praise and Thank God for Life

"Why do I have to say my prayers every morning?" a sleepy Maria asked her mother as she got ready for school.

"Think of all the good things God has given us," her mother answered. "Each morning we praise God for the new day, and we praise God for giving us life."

"I'm so glad God has given me Nana and Papa and you, too, Mommy," smiled Maria.

"That's the idea, Maria," Mother replied. Then she said, "Would you like to learn the prayer I say? Each morning I pray,

"O God, I praise You
    for giving us this new day.
I praise You for giving me life today.
I ask Your blessing on all that I do
    and say. Amen."

That night just before Maria went to bed, her mother hugged her and said, "Let's say our night prayers together, Maria. At night we thank God for all the gifts of the day. What do you want to thank God for?"

Maria said, "I thank God for my good friend, Bridget. I thank God for my family. And I thank God that I could read my story without any help when my teacher asked me to read today."

Mother said, "At night we also ask God to forgive us for whatever we did during the day that was wrong. Do you need to ask God to forgive you for anything?"

"Well," Maria said slowly, "I did get mad at Brian when he yelled at me. Then I pushed him so I could get in front of him in the lunch line. I'm sorry that I pushed Brian. I will try to be nice to him tomorrow."

"That was a good prayer," said Mother as she blessed Maria on the forehead. "Good night, Sweetie. Sleep tight!"

Christians praise God in morning prayer.
We praise God because life is good.
We praise God for giving us a new day.
We ask God to be with us during the day.
We ask God to help us love and serve others.

What will you praise God for
in your morning prayers?
How will you love and serve others?
Draw what you will do here.

Christians thank God in night prayer.
We thank God for giving us
the blessings of the day.
We ask God to protect us
through the night.
We ask forgiveness for the things
we have done wrong.
We thank God for giving us life.

Here is a prayer to say at night.

O God, thank You
    for all the good things I did today.
Bless all the people
    who helped me today.
Thank You for giving me life.
Forgive me for whatever I did wrong today.
Protect me through the night.
Amen.

Decorate your prayer.
Can you learn this prayer by heart?

Let Us Pray

Catechist: We learned some prayers to thank God for all our blessings.
Now let us make up some of our own thank-you prayers.
When I thank God for the wonderful things God has given us,
we will sing, "I am wonderfully made."
Thank You, God, for eyes that wink.

All sing: I am wonderfully made.

Catechist: Thank You, God, for hands that clap.

All sing: I am wonderfully made.

Catechist: May God bless you as you work and play.
May God give you friends,
and rainbows and sunshine.
May God be with you
while you are on summer vacation.

All: Amen.

Remembering

Read with Me

Write the best answer on each blank.

1. The greatest part of God's creation is _____.

    the sun   people

2. Jesus tells us we will be happy if we love and help _____.

    the animals   other people

3. God wants people to care for God's _____.

    Son   creation

4. We share the gift of life when we treat _____ people fairly.

    some   all

5. Jesus tells us we will be _____ if we show our love for God.

    happy   sad

6. We _____ God in our morning prayers.

    bless   praise

7. We _____ God in our night prayers.

    bless   thank

Advent/Christmas

Advent is a time for getting ready. We get ready to celebrate the birthday of Jesus. We celebrate Jesus' birth on December 25, the feast we call Christmas.

Jesus was born many, many years ago. He was sent by God to live with us. Jesus is God's Son. We call Jesus "Emmanuel." <u>Emmanuel</u> means "God with us."

During Advent we remember that God gave us the greatest of all gifts, Jesus. We get ready to thank God for this great gift. We get ready to celebrate Jesus' birthday.

Jesus was born just as we were. He died, and God raised Jesus from the dead. Jesus Christ is always with us.

Advent is a time to get ready to celebrate Jesus' birth and life. During Advent we remember that Jesus is always with us.

Prayer

Catechist: We know Jesus is with us when we come together to pray. We call Jesus "Emmanuel" because He is always with us. Let us sing our special Advent song.

Jesus is with us in the good things we do for others. During this Advent season we prepare to celebrate Jesus' birth in Bethlehem many years ago.

John the Baptizer was sent by God to help people prepare for the coming of Jesus. Let us listen to what the gospel tells us about John.

All stand and sing: Alleluia!

Reader: John was the man the prophet Isaiah was talking about when he said, "Someone is shouting in the desert, 'Prepare a road for the Lord; make a straight path for him to travel!'"
(Matthew 3:3)

Catechist: During these days let us prepare to celebrate the coming of Jesus.

All: Come, Lord Jesus.

Catechist: We ask our God to bless us as we pray.

All: In the name of the Father . . .

Easter

The resurrection of Jesus is the great Christian feast. On every Sunday we celebrate the resurrection of Jesus. But we celebrate Jesus' resurrection in a special way on Easter Sunday.

At Easter Christians sing **"Alleluia! Alleluia!"** Alleluia means "Praise God!"

We praise God for raising Jesus from the dead. In the resurrection God gave Jesus new life.

At Easter we praise God who will raise us from the dead. We hope we will live a new life with Jesus.

Baptism is a sign of our new life with Jesus. Each time the Church baptizes a child or an adult, the baptized person shares in the Easter life of Jesus.

In our parishes Easter is a time for baptisms. New people become members of our community, the Church. When they are baptized, they share in the life of Jesus. Through baptism we all share in God's life.

Alleluia! Alleluia! Alleluia!

Prayer

Catechist: We gather here at the baptismal font to praise the Risen Christ and to pray for those who were recently baptized.

All sing: Alleluia! Alleluia!

Catechist: Let us listen to the gospel story of Jesus talking to Martha.

All stand and sing: Alleluia! Alleluia!

Reader: Many people came to comfort Martha and Mary about their brother's death. Martha said to Jesus, "My brother would not have died if you had been here!" Jesus told her, "Your brother will rise to life. I am the resurrection and the life." (From John 11:19-25)

All: Alleluia! Alleluia!

Reader: The gospel of the Lord.

All: Praise to you, Lord Jesus Christ.

Catechist: Today we pray for those people who were recently baptized. As I call their names, please bring up your cards and place them on the table.

Let us close with our Easter song.

All sing: Alleluia! Alleluia!

Prayers

The Sign of the Cross
In the name of the Father,
and of the Son,
and of the Holy Spirit. Amen.

The Lord's Prayer
Our Father, who art in heaven,
hallowed be thy name.
Thy Kingdom come.
Thy will be done on earth
as it is in heaven.
Give us this day our daily bread,
and forgive us our trespasses
as we forgive those who trespass
against us.
And lead us not into temptation,
but deliver us from evil. Amen.

Hail Mary
Hail Mary, full of grace,
the Lord is with you.
Blessed are you among women,
and blessed is the fruit
of your womb, Jesus.
Holy Mary, Mother of God,
pray for us sinners,
now and at the hour of our death.
Amen.

The Glory Prayer
Glory to the Father,
and to the Son,
and to the Holy Spirit:
as it was in the beginning, is now
and will be for ever. Amen.

Señal de la Cruz
En el nombre del Padre
y del Hijo
y del Espíritu Santo. Amén.

Padre Nuestro
Padre nuestro, que estás en el cielo.
Santificado sea tu nombre.
Venga tu reino.
Hágase tu voluntad en la tierra
como en el cielo.
Danos hoy nuestro pan de cada día.
Perdona nuestra ofensas, como
también nosotros perdonamos a
los que nos ofenden.
No nos dejes caer en tentación,
y líbranos del mal. Amén.

Ave María
Dios te salve, María, llena eres
de gracia, el Señor es contigo,
bendita tú eres entre todas las
mujeres, y bendito es el fruto
de tu vientre, Jesús.
Santa María, Madre de Dios,
ruega por nosotros los pecadores,
ahora y en la hora de nuestra
muerte. Amén.

Gloria al Padre
Gloria al Padre, y al Hijo,
y al Espíritu Santo.
Como era en el principio, ahora y
siempre, por los siglos de los siglos.
Amén.